ISAIAS: MAN OF IDEAS

ISAIAS:

Man of Ideas

By

DOM HUBERT VAN ZELLER

THE NEWMAN PRESS
WESTMINSTER, MARYLAND
1951

First Published 1938
Reprinted 1951

NIHIL OBSTAT:

JUSTIN McCANN, O.S.B.,
Censor.

IMPRIMATUR:

W. E. KELLY,
Ab. Pres.

NIHIL OBSTAT:

GEORGIUS CAN. SMITH, S.TH.D., PH.D.,
Censor deputatus.

IMPRIMATUR:

LEONELLUS CAN. EVANS,
Vic. Gen.

WESTMONASTERII,
die 11a Januarii 1938.

Printed in the United States of America

DEDICATION

Dear David,

 So that you may not think that the prophets were all of them stern men, bleak and rock-face in the manner of their approach to God, I dedicate to you my understanding—such as it is—of Isaias.

When reading about these heroes of the Old Testament, people are apt to get hold of the wrong end—the Calvinist end—of the stick. Perhaps this is because those who write about the prophets are mostly holding the stick upside down. Or, alternatively, perhaps it is because they are standing on their heads. At any rate, I am sure that if you laymen were more Bible-proud than you are, we clerics would make ourselves better understood than we do —I mean about the Scriptures. You see, at present we hardly dare to spend much time upon the Old Testament in our sermons ; we are afraid that our references will not be recognized. We are also afraid—I confess it—of not being thought very interesting and fresh.

Anyway, here you have Isaias. *I* find him ' interesting ' *and* ' fresh.' If you don't find him ' interesting ' and ' fresh ' then the fault is yours. Or—more probably— mine. But not his.

Constantly yours,

Downside, 1937.   H. v Z.

CONTENTS

ACKNOWLEDGEMENT

AMONG the authorities consulted, those that have helped me most and to whom I hereby express my gratitude, are the following :

Cheyne, *Isaiah ;* Driver, *Isaiah, His Life and Times ;* Goodier, *About the Old Testament ;* Lods, *The Prophets and the Rise of Judaism ;* Pope, *The Catholic Student's ' Aids' to the Bible ;* Smith, *The Prophets of Israel ;* Sayce, *The Times of Isaiah ;* and *The Cambridge Companion to the Bible.*

* * *

No passage in this book is to be interpreted in any sense other than that accepted by the Holy See of Rome.

O Almighty and Eternal God, the only hope of the world, who by the preaching of Thy Prophets hast declared the mysteries of this present time, graciously increase the devotion of Thy people, since none of the faithful can advance in virtue without Thy inspiration. *Collect after the twelfth prophecy of Holy Saturday.*

One of the old men used to say : ' The Prophets compiled the Scriptures, and the Fathers have copied them, and the men who came after them learned to repeat them by heart ; then hath come this generation that hath placed them in cupboards.' *The Paradise of the Fathers*, Vol. II, Bk. I, Ch. VIII.

ISAIAS: MAN OF IDEAS

CHAPTER I

INTRODUCTORY

IT would be very convenient if, in order to arrive at
an estimate of the Prophet's career, we could simply
take his book chapter by chapter until a farewell
message were arrived at in the concluding verses.
But to such a measured process Isaias refuses, unfortunately, to yield. Commentators and historians
have, for the most part, chosen to look at the Prophecy
of Isaias from the various angles into which Juda's
political situation happens to have forced the author
at different times ; thus we have in the standard textbooks such divisions as 'Isaias and the Assyrian
Problem,' 'Isaias and the Egyptian Problem,' 'The
Home Policy of Isaias' and so on, which, supposing
the desire to study the period scientifically, is undoubtedly the best way of going about it, but which
is, for the reader who asks for a few facts about the
Prophet and a surface grasp of his work, a method
that is inclined to smother the central figure. The
ins and outs of Juda's troubled eighth-century history
are so complicated that to take the reader behind the
thrones of Babylon, Niniveh, and Damascus would
mean the survey of about three centuries of history
and about four feet of map, so that in the end (if the

reader is the kind of person I think he is—namely, one with tendencies like my own) the only part of the book not to be skipped would turn out to be that dealing with the bare seventy years of the Prophet's career, while the only part of the map to be studied would be that covering the Juda area.

I will thus depart from the method of the lecture-hall and take my stand by the system of the school-room : reign by reign will be considered, and Isaias's activities in each ; the Prophet will be allowed to cope with the separate political problems as they come up. On the face of it this looks simplicity itself, and the reader is doubtless settling down to the comforting thought that no great strain is being asked of him, and that dates, names, and dynasties can go their own sweet way unheeded. . . So it is only fair to say (lest the pages that follow should be looked upon as children's-corner material) that in any sort of understanding of Isaias *some* knowledge of local history is needed for background. Key names—apart from those of Juda's leaders—will occur again and again, and unless the reader becomes moderately familiar with the personalities that bore them he will miss much of the significance of Isaias's attitude towards them. In fact the more we get to know the characters of any historical drama the better—even if these characters are in the wings most of the time and are being spoken of with bated breath by those who occupy the stage. After all, what is there that separates us from Sargon or Salmanasar that does not also separate us from, say, Hitler or Mussolini ? Time, nothing more than that. Do we understand the dictator Ataturk any better than we understand the dictator Cyrus ? Outside his family, and apart of

course from the knowledge possessed by the proverbial
valet, there is little enough that is known of any
public figure. But just as a modern political memoir
will make deadly reading without some acquaintance
of the characters that are introduced, so the following
pages are liable to be chill indeed if the Phacees, the
Rasins, the Sennacheribs, and the Theglathphalasars
are dropped by the way.

Which brings me to a further point : this book is
not a ' political memoir.' I hesitate to say what I
think it is, but I am quite sure that it is not that.
Nor is it a summary, in popular form, of Juda's
vacillating allegiances ; neither is it a Bible-made-
easy book (or made ' funny,' or made ' controversial ') ;
nor yet is it written to support pet theories of my own.

Isaias is more than a statesman, he is a saint ;
the Bible is more than a collection of belles-lettres, it
is the word of God. The prophecies we are about to
examine are not a series of little essays of long ago—
' warmly to be recommended to the reader ' by me—
they are timeless, cosmic, self-recommended. . . .
They are what was written, published, promulgated
by the Holy Spirit Himself. If anyone is inclined to
doubt the fact he had better not read what I have to
say. So it comes to this, that what I do and what you
do, dear reader, in our several approaches to the
Prophecy of Isaias is of very little moment : what
either of us does is to be measured only by the
reverence with which we do it. And now for the
Prophet Isaias.

.   .   .   .   .   .

' The vision of Isaias the son of Amos, which he
saw concerning Juda and Jerusalem in the days of

Ozias, Joatham, Achaz, and Ezechias, kings of Juda.'
In this brief exordium we find, as suggested above, the
plan or scheme which will best assist us in allotting
the material of our subject's biography : the kingly
line of Juda.   Whatever uncertainty may exist on
other points, there can be no doubt about the Prophet's
period. He began to prophesy in, roughly, 742 B.C. at
the time when Ozias was plotting against his Assyrian
neighbour, and he ceased to prophesy in (again roughly)
700 when the reign of Ezechias, the fourth succeeding
king, was drawing to a close.   As this gives Isaias
about forty years of active prophetical labours we can
make him between sixty and seventy years old when
he came to die ; it is hardly likely that he began
prophesying before he was twenty, and it is certain
that he added nothing to his book in the reign of
Ezechias's successor, Manasses. In fact it is commonly
held at the present time that Isaias was already dead
by the time that Manasses ascended the throne. If
this was so then we have to forget the legend that has
been believed for many centuries regarding the manner
of the Prophet's death—that he was sawn in two at
the order of Manasses.

If you take it that Isaias died at the end of Ezechias's
reign you have a picture of a happy finish to the
Prophet's hard-run course ; if you believe (as I do,
though I shall make no attempt to make you join me
in this because I have not a shred of evidence) that
tradition has more to be said for it than have the
doubtful opinions of certain divines, then I am afraid
you have Isaias dying a disappointed man.   With
Ezechias still on the throne the threats of the Prophet
were showing signs of being vindicated, the hopes of
the Prophet were showing signs of having something

in them after all. . . But with the first years of
Manasses, on the other hand, it would have looked to
the dying Prophet—dying in a tree-trunk, with the
teeth of a saw in his stomach—that all his work had
been reversed and all his dreams had been exploded.
No, perhaps not that ; Isaias was a man of faith and
so, at worst, he would have regarded his work—God's
work—as having suffered an eclipse. But we are
beginning at the wrong end : Isaias's origins, not his
obsequies, must be considered here. One word more
before we pick him up in the reign of an earlier king :
even if we take the sawn-in-two version as sheer
fable, the fact that the Prophet's name is so
dramatically linked with that of Manasses seems to
suggest that the two men were at loggerheads with one
another, come what did at the end of it. But far be
it from me to claim that the Prophet was not already
dead long ago.

Isaias's origins then : who was he ? He says in the
superscription just quoted that ' Amos ' was his father's
name. As far as I know, no one has ever tried to prove
that this is the Amos of the Prophecy that bears that
name ; Isaias's father has, however, been identified
with ' Amazias,' the predecessor of King Ozias, and
again with a younger brother of the same sovereign.
Both associations seem wildly improbable. If the
Prophet's father was a king, why does he not say so ?
If Amos was Amazias's brother would there not have
been confusion at home : Amos meaning ' He is
strong ' and Amazias, ' The Lord is strong ' ? Though
it is fairly frequent to find brothers in the East bearing
much the same name it is usually seen to be with some
more marked qualification than this. If we look in
other directions altogether for a clue to the pedigree

B

of Isaias, there exists a pre-Exilic Hebrew seal which
refers to a certain Amos ' the scribe.' But there must
have been dozens of scribes called Amos. The fact of
the matter is that we have nothing whatever to
indicate *who* Isaias's father was ; for the royal-blood
theory we have nothing more than Rabbinical
authority, and to connect Amos with anyone else we
have no authority at all.

But royal or not royal, an interesting side-light is
thrown upon the social standing of Isaias by the late
Dr. Sayce who quotes 2 Kings xx, 4 (R.V.) to show
that Isaias, in leaving the palace for the ' middle city,'
was going home towards that part of the town which
was occupied by the residential classes. The Temple
stood on Mount Moriah, *above* Ezechias's palace, so
the Prophet was not one of those officials who dwelt
within the sacred enclosure, nor was his house in the
' lower city ' which was mostly occupied by the working
classes and the small tradesmen. It is only a hint, no
more. But even if we get nothing very certain either
way as witness to the blueness or the redness of the
Prophet's blood, the internal evidence of his book would
seem to prove that, if not actually an aristocrat, Isaias
was at any rate a cultivated man. We must remember
that the Prophet stood at the elbows of four kings in
succession, speaking to them as an equal (if not as a
tutor), so it is hardly likely that he was of peasant or
provincial stock ; genius for statesmanship may lift a
man to positions he would not have dreamed of when
he started out on his career, but it does not introduce
its possessors to royal intimacy without a struggle.

Whatever the circumstances of his birth, Isaias
certainly had the freedom of the court long before he
had justified his existence as a courtier. One ventures

to think, in fact, reading between the lines, that it was because of his rank that he was able to say about religion all that he did ; where the words of a professional preacher or theologian would have been submitted to a discount of about thirty per cent, the words of Isaias the aristocratic layman were accepted at more or less face value. We shall notice as we trace the Prophet's course that in making him more of a man of God Isaias's ' vision ' made him no less of a diplomat. To *him*, yes, the prophetical vocation made all the difference in the world—supernaturalizing every movement on the board—but to the kings whom he advised, and to the men in the street with whom he walked, there was probably very little difference at the beginning, between Isaias and any other minister of the crown. . . . Here was a nobleman (first), who was a prophet (second) ; a particularly upright nobleman, of course, and possibly a mute reproach to sundry others of the court, but . . . well, one would have expected something rather special from one who was also endowed with very definite supernatural gifts. And then, as time wore on and as king succeeded king, there would be an unconscious change of attitude towards the Prophet : here was a prophet (first), who happened to be exceedingly astute in foreign politics (second).

Isaias was married and had at least two children. The eldest boy, Jasub, accompanied his father at the Lord's command (vii, 3) when the famous interview took place between the Prophet and King Achaz at the ' conduit of the upper pool.' So this son, Jasub, must have been born fairly soon after the accession of Achaz. The birth of the second child, Marshalalhabaz, would have taken place (viii, 3) shortly before the

downfall of Samaria. In the names of both these
children, as in the name of Isaias himself—Isaias
means ' Salvation of the Lord '—there is more than a
chance significance. ' Shear-jasub,' or ' Jasub ' as he
is referred to by the Lord, is the Hebrew for ' A
remnant shall return '—a hope which the boy's father
had constantly to keep before his eyes ; so constantly,
in fact, does this idea of a faithful few who will survive
recur in the message of Isaias that the naming of his
first-born is no certain clue to the date of the event :
each new menace to Juda's peace was met by the
Prophet with ' Shear-jasub ' ; ' I tell you,' said Isaias
in effect, ' to trust in God. You won't do it. Very
well, I'm afraid that most of you will perish as a result.
Still, *a remnant shall return.*' We shall hear the same
kind of thing again and again. But to return to
Jasub : if that little person was old enough to toddle
along at his father's side and to attend the discussion
with Achaz, then—putting it at its latest—he must
have been born a year or so before his brother, or—
putting it at its earliest—during the concluding years
of Joatham's reign—round about 740.

The name of the second son was the herald of its
birth (viii, 1). The Lord told Isaias (viii, 3) that the
child was to be called ' Hasten to take away the spoils,
make haste to take away the prey.' This name, or
rather the slightly shortened form of it, ' Spoil quickly,
rob swiftly,' was inscribed in a ' large book '—again at
the Lord's injunction—and with ' a man's pen ' so
that all the world might be aware of the fact. The
Revised Version has ' large slab ' and ' graver's tool '
instead of the book and pen, implying that the message
—not of the child's birth but of the precarious state of
affairs in Juda—was so important that it was worth

while carving it indelibly in stone. But from the child's point of view, what a name to come into the world with! I like to think of him in later years wandering towards the market-place or Temple precincts, and gazing at the crude lettering which spelt his own name. Perhaps by that time the people of Jerusalem had forgotten how the words had come to be written, perhaps they hardly ever looked up to the niche in the wall where the 'slab' had been placed (so does familiarity blunt the sense), but 'at all events' Marshalalhabaz reflects, 'there can't be many people in Palestine with a name like that!' How his elder brother must have teased him! And we can imagine the mother, whom Isaias styles 'the prophetess,' grimly repeating the first part of the name as she picks up the mending basket at the end of the week . . . 'Spoil quickly. Or we can think of the second part of the name, 'Rob swiftly,' as it is whispered to the poor child by some horrid little schoolboy . . . ' so *that's* why you always seem to have new toys . . .

But perhaps most readily of all it is Isaias's own name that we can hear whispered over the centuries . . . 'Salvation of the Lord' . . . how he must have gloried in it! Like that of his eldest son, here was a title, a hope, a boast. Here was a text that spelt ultimate triumph, here was a text that contained the sum of all the Prophet's doctrine, here was the goal to which he was leading an obstinate race. That Jehovah should bring redemption to His faithless children—that He should Himself *be* that redemption —is the very burden of Isaias's Prophecy. A salvation which is to follow a practical extinction forms the material of all the Prophet's earlier preaching; later

he will tell of the manner of that salvation's coming :
he will sound the trumpet of the Gospel, he will tell
of the Coming of the Christ.

If Salvation is one of the names of the Messias, then
the herald-prophet of Christ is fittingly called ' Salvation of the Lord.' More clearly than any other prophet
does Isaias proclaim the promise of the New Law ; he
seems to see over the shoulders of his own age—over
the shoulders, even, of our own—announcing to all
mankind the finality of the Gospel sway, universal,
vindicated, undenied.

Thus in the course of this essay it will be seen (I
hope) how much more of an evangelist is Isaias than
are his fellow-prophets. Not surprising, therefore,
that the Church links together, at the most solemn
seasons of the liturgical year, the Old Testament and
the New by freely drawing from Isaias's Prophecy.
Isaias is the Arch-Prophet, the Prophet whose title
rests simply on his ' vision ', and not on his personality
or power of working miracles. Where an Elias or an
Eliseus may be said to owe his success to the gifts of
God, Isaias is felt to owe all to God Himself. Oh, yes,
he had his share of individuality ; gifted, was Isaias,
with natural talent quite beyond the ordinary as we
shall see ; miracles, too, were part, one might say,
of the Prophet's stock-in-trade—witness the cure
of the sovereign's boil—but it was as an announcer
of God's Messianic Message, a more *spiritual* message than any that had been announced before,
that Isaias gave the traditional part of prophet a
new rendering.

This brings us to what the Prophet actually said
that was in any sense new. How did he differ, for
example, from the other almost contemporary prophets

in Israel, Amos and Osee ? Or even from his own countryman, Joel ? Like every prophet worthy of the name, Isaias will be heard to thunder against the particular evils of the day : we shall find him accusing the rich of oppressing the poor, we shall listen to his scornful denunciation of the self-indulgent, the smugly satisfied, the outwardly-righteous-but-inwardly-corrupt, we shall see him lifting the veil to expose the rotting juridical system . . . but it is his confidence in God and his confidence in the foundations of Jerusalem —attitudes which are not merely negative—that show us the real Isaias. He is so convinced that the Lord is looking after Juda that it is as much as he can do, when Juda's sins are coming up for censure, to keep to the point. The stone of Sion is God-placed, Jerusalem is rooted for good and all . . . this it is that marks Isaias from contemporary or future prophets.

So if, in the reading of our Prophet, there is one verse before all others which it would be well to learn by heart (allowing that the reader is willing to follow my finger down Isaias's page) it is v. 16 of ch. xxviii : ' Therefore thus saith the Lord God : Behold I will lay a stone in the foundations of Sion, a tried stone, a corner stone, a precious stone, founded in the foundation. He that believeth, let him not hasten.' However upset are the fortunes of Israel there is always *that* to be thankful for—Sion is ' precious ' in the sight of God. Sion is ' founded,' and God does not waste the foundations He has made. All this is an earnest, surely, of the Messias who is to come . . . and of the Church He is to found. The ' stone ' of Isaias's Prophecy is a figure which will become still more familiar in the days of the Lord whose advent is heralded here. ' Upon this rock,' says Our Lord, ' I will build My Church ;

and the gates of hell shall not prevail against it.' As permanent is Peter as the Church itself . . . and Christ and the Church—the New Jerusalem—are One.

This idea, which we might call the ' stone-motif,' would have been especially acceptable to the Prophet's hearers on account of its association with the building of the Temple. We do not have to know very much about the books of the Old Testament to remember the frequency with which references to ecclesiastical architecture occur ; to the Jews the Temple was the symbol of centralization, stability, constitutional religion. The key-thought, then, which the Prophet keeps ever before his remarkably well-stocked mind, is, undoubtedly, that of the *establishment* of the Chosen People ; or, to put it in another way and going one step further, his is the doctrine of the Longsightedness of God. Again and again we hear the Prophet reminding his opportunist and expedient-grasping flock that if only they will fix their hopes in *God* and not in political alliances of the moment—or indeed in human securities of any kind—they will be perfectly safe ; God cares for them.

' You Jews ' (might be the summing up of all Isaias's doctrine in a single speech) ' are constitutionally indestructible ; as long as you look to your Founder you will want for nothing. By casting about for temporal support you are being *untrue* to your con- stitution. Your existence as a nation depends, and always has depended, on God alone. Give up God and you kick away your foundation-stone. But God will not suffer Himself to be so kicked away. He has founded you on, and in, Himself. And as for these dangers that threaten, dangers that are here to-day and gone to-morrow, dangers which seem to imperil your

national life but which somehow or other are always
averted at the last moment . . . are not these dangers
meant? Did not God say a "*tried*" stone? Believe
me ' (so might Isaias go on), ' these impending menaces
of which you are afraid do to your national life nothing
like the harm that is done by your turning to the
insurance policies of your neighbours. It is not your
foes that are your greatest danger, your real enemies
are yourselves.' And then there is the final ' He that
hath faith shall not make haste.' This winding up is
really a winding up; it is not a stray remark that has
nothing to do with the foregoing; it is a very earnest
piece of advice arising out of what the Prophet has
just been talking about. Oh, it is not only to the
pusillanimous Jews that this little maxim is addressed!
It is to you, gentle reader, and to me. ' He that hath
faith ' . . . if only we really *believed* that we were
' precious ' to God, precious in spite of our meannesses
and grudging services, precious for no merit of our own
but simply because ' He hath first loved us ' . . . If
only we *believed* that we were resting on ' solid foundation '—even when we seemed to be hanging on to the
face of a cliff with nothing much more than our finger-
nails—if only we could appreciate in practice and not
merely on paper that to be ' tried ' was all part of the
plan . . . would we be so eager to ' make haste '?
The fault is, of course, the very obvious one which
is at the bottom of all discouragement, and of most
sins, namely that we forget about the Eternity of God
and remember only the interminable boredom of our
own lives. Either through impatience or panic we grasp
at the easy solution; we stop short half-way. We
claim—without perhaps formulating our ' strike ' in
any such glaring terms—that if God will not see to

our interests *we* must attend to them, ' God helps
those who help themselves,' etc. ; He may do, but is
He not far more inclined to help those who trust in
Him ?   Sometimes we go even further and act as if
God *could* not see to His interests—His *own* interests
—let alone the interests of His creatures !   We busy
ourselves with correcting His work—*His* work, if you
please—excusing ourselves all along that it is precisely
because it is His work and not our own that we are
doing so.   There is not much harm perhaps in designing
the works of God—if human plans happen to coincide
with the plans of Providence they will come to something, otherwise not—but there is a great deal of harm
in trying to force the Will of God into boundaries of
our own making.   Sinners commit sin and know where
they are in the matter ;   good people neglect grace and
fall into all kinds of delusions.   Why ?   Because they
know—or think—that they are good.   ' At any cost,'
says the good man, ' God's work must be furthered.
So-and-so is reprobate because he doesn't fit in.   Such-
and-such a change must be made because who ever
heard of God's work with that sort of thing going on ?
In fact, just to show how good I am, and how much I
have the work of God at heart, I will change my whole
self.'   And so the thing goes on . . . and by the end it
is no longer the work of God that is done, but simply
the work of self.

' O soul,' would be the advice of Isaias to him who
would force the pace of God, ' remember the centuries
that the eyes of God have seen.   Recall the generations
that are yet to come.   Be still, there is plenty of time.
Look at life, O soul—your life and the life of mankind
at large—through the eyes of God.   God's plan frus-
trated ?   Oh no !   only a long time being realized !

What does it matter if you—little, inconsiderable, but infinitely-precious-in-God's-sight *you*—are unable to see the results of your work ? For whom is the work being done ? Is it not for God ? Well, then, results will follow in due time . . . perhaps a fortnight before you die, perhaps two, three, four centuries after ! It doesn't matter, there is plenty of time.' So, I think, would Isaias have spoken to us ' hasteners '. He would have had us understand the massiveness of God, and in the largeness of the Divine Heart he would have had us see our pettiness, our impatience, and our greed. But he would also have had us see our preciousness.

CHAPTER II

IN OZIAS'S REIGN

I CALL him ' Ozias ' because that is what Isaias calls him in the opening verse of the Prophecy ; the king in question is as freely referred to as ' Azarias '—a fact which is worth remembering when looking up the Fourth Book of Kings for corroboration of what is given in the appropriate passages of Isaias. Here the chapters to be taken together are : Isaias vi, 4 Kings xv.

Ozias was the son of Amazias. He followed his father on the throne of Juda somewhere in the region of 765 and he died somewhere in the region of 740. The dates of these kings have never been satisfactorily established ; it will be seen that I have gone upon the principle of advancing the reigns of most sovereigns by about ten or fifteen years on what was believed to be correct at the end of the last century. I think I have the leading Catholic authorities with me in this.

' In the year that King Ozias died,' says the Prophet, ' I saw the Lord, etc.,' and then he gives his vision. So when I write at the head of this chapter ' *in* Ozias's reign,' I really mean, if the interests of accuracy are to be preserved, ' right at the end of ' . . . but, of course, I naturally want to get in all the reigns I can. Now let us examine the Prophet's vision.

The vision seems to have been granted in the Temple

itself. God appeared in Person. The description is as follows : ' I saw God sitting upon a throne high and elevated, and His train filled the Temple. Upon it stood the seraphims : the one had six wings, the other had six wings : with two they covered His face, and with two they covered His feet, and with two they flew. And they cried one to another and said : Holy, Holy, Holy, the Lord God of Hosts, all the earth is full of His glory. And the lintels of the doors were moved at the voice of him that cried ; and the house was filled with smoke.'

Now Isaias knew that it was not granted to man to ' see God and live,' so, having seen God, he fully expected to die. ' Woe is me,' he cried, ' I am undone.'[1] But before being wiped out of existence he was determined to make two points clear (though to whom he was making them clear is not, on the face of it, obvious : was he talking to God ? to the seraphims ? to his own soul ?). The text continues as follows : ' Because I am a man of unclean lips and I dwell in the midst of a people that hath unclean lips.' St. Peter's ' depart from me, O Lord, for I am a sinful man ' is an echo of this protestation on Isaias's part. But the Prophet goes one further than the Apostle—he says that nobody else is worthy either. In fact one seems to see in Isaias more of hopelessness and diffidence than of true humility ; in the call of Peter it was the healthy sense of shame that prompted the remark. Peter would have been horrified if Our Lord *had* departed from him. In the case of Isaias it would appear that by some instant flash of intuition he was given to

---

[1] Our version has : ' Woe is me, because I have held my peace.' Ordinarily I use our version, and will make a point of saying so on the rare occasions when I do not ; the words of the Revised Version seem in this place to be more expressive.

understand what was required of him ; the prophetical
vocation was held out, his hour was come, a choice
had to be made. . . . (Rarely are these graces *forced*
upon the soul ; the will is nearly always given the
chance of meriting by the right use of its freedom.)
Well, what happened ? In that split instant of light
Isaias seems to have come to the conclusion that God
didn't *really* know His own business, and that what
God wanted could not, under the existing circumstances, be satisfactorily brought about : ' The work
of God will never prosper in my hands because I am a
sinner. And as a matter of fact the work of God will
never prosper anyway, because those for whom it is
worked are sinners also.' That was roughly what was
passing through the mind of Isaias when he spoke
of ' unclean lips ' : he was telling God (or the
seraphims, or himself) that two wrongs could not
make a right . . . and that therefore the simplest
thing would be for him to follow the ordinary
law and drop down dead as the result of having ' seen
the Lord.'

So you see why I made such a point in the last chapter
of not dictating God's duties to God. Once that truth
was firmly rooted in the Prophet's mind, he brought
it out—in different forms—whenever he preached to
the Jews the doctrine of submission. It is here at the
outset, in the actual call of Isaias to the service of
God, that I would like to think of him learning that
lesson. The way in which God dealt with him in the
matter is instructive :

' And one of the seraphims flew to me ; and in his
hand was a live coal which he had taken with the tongs
off the altar. And he touched my mouth and said :
Behold this hath touched thy lips, and thy iniquities

shall be taken away, and thy sin shall be cleansed.'
So the big objection is disposed of ! In the twinkling
of an eye the *natural* disqualifications, the accumulated
weaknesses of a lifetime, those hundred-and-one little
defects and hesitations which keep back the soul from
grasping the hand that is held out to it . . . all are rolled
away in the magnificent sweep of grace. The trouble,
of course, with most of us is that we cannot *see* ourselves as anything but what we are. It is not that we
pit our strength against the strength of God—to do so
would obviously be madness—it is rather that we drag
out our ' personalities,' our congenital inhibitions, our
ingrained dispositions, and place them between ourselves and God. We are so afraid of the vision of what
we ought to be that we prefer to look at the picture of
what we are. But God can change that picture, it is
only painted in human colours. He will not destroy
it . . . He may not even take it from its frame. He
will paint over it, or draw to the surface the colour
that is there.

' And I heard the voice of the Lord saying : Whom
shall I send, and who shall go for us ? And I said :
Lo, here am I, send me. And He said : Go, and thou
shalt say to this people : Hearing, hear and understand not ; and see the vision and know it not.' And
then the Lord goes on to give further evidence of the
hardness of heart with which the Prophet's preaching
will be met.

Now this description of God taking counsel with the
hosts of Heaven, of seraphims whose voices shake
the earth, of coals being snatched from the altar
to do their healing work, is no mere fairy story.
It is an incident that is referred to in the
prayers of the Mass. It may read like a Dunsany

apocalypse, but we are nevertheless to take it literally.

'And I heard the Lord saying : Whom shall I send ? ' This is all terribly vivid, but more than that it is a striking instance of the way in which the Lord holds out to over-diffident souls another chance. God, by letting Isaias overhear the consultation which He is having with His elect, is enticing His servant to offer himself after all. It is the same grace as the first appeal, only it comes in a slightly different—and probably a stronger—form. Where the former call seems to have shed light upon the work which was to be done, and its unpleasantness, this second invitation seems to have appealed to the Prophet's generosity. We are always far more approachable when our capacity for heroism is drawn upon than when a certain task is simply put before us. In Isaias's case, the objective method having failed, it was for the subjective method to bring out what was best in him. True, it was a call on a slightly lower key, but such is the merciful way of God : He does not ask us to do *harder* things when once we fail Him, He asks us to do easier ones . . . and then, when we are sufficiently practised in doing the easy works, He honours us again by putting before us something difficult.

'And I said : Lo, here am I, send me ! ' Isaias rises magnificently to the occasion ! What one might call the ' ruse ' of God has worked. Commentators speak truly when they draw attention to the ' daring ' of Isaias. He was brave, obviously, when he volunteered for a work which was probably hidden from him (because, though he may have seen what was wanted of him in the first call, in the second he saw

only that he was wanted[1]), but he was distinctly more
' daring '—in the sense that pioneers of literature and
art are ' daring '—when he recorded the manner of his
initiation. One wonders how the Jews of Isaias's own
time regarded this passage. The first part of the
account would have meant far more to them than it
does to us, but they would have been rather staggered
by the second part. The Hebrew Temple-goer—far
more Scripture-conscious than his Christian counter-
part of the present day—would have revelled in the
tremendous solemnity of the Prophet's opening
strophes ; there was meaning in ' the throne high and
elevated,' in the train which ' filled the Temple,' in
the ' winged seraphim,' the ' smoke which filled the
House of God,' the ' shaking of the lintels ' . . . And
then the sudden change, the almost homely intimacy
of the second part of the story : God revealing His
difficulties out loud ! God letting Himself be over-
heard by mortal man ! Perhaps the Jews understood
this sort of thing better than we do, I do not know,
but it seems to me distinctly ' daring '. God is represented here as *pretending* to a problem which, in His
case, cannot possibly arise. He is shown as rehearsing
a scene, as forcing a situation. Well, one thing we can
derive from it is the impression of the lengths to which
the Lord is prepared to go in eliciting the free-will
offering of His creatures. In the Old Testament God
does not often stoop to conquer—that is the message of

[1] I would venture to suggest that the reason for a soul's inability
to see *now* what it saw a moment ago might be found in the fact
that darkness follows infidelity—however slight. It might be
objected that here God seems to have given *more* light instead of
less. . . . Yes, but it was light on another subject ; and for this
light to be seen it was necessary for the other to have been withdrawn ; for the other was the greater light. The point is at least
arguable.

the New—but here we have Him anxious about a man, anxious that Isaias should miss nothing of the favours extended to his soul. It is sublime . . . as Divine Condescension is inevitably sublime.

Thus we can see even now, before we have read a dozen verses of his text, that Isaias is more ' New Testament ' than his fellows. It is for him to tell us of the God of Love, tender and inviting a return of love ; here is the Lord who will reveal Himself as the Good Shepherd ; Jehovah considering and considerate. Isaias, with all his ideas, has but one idea—the idea of Love. It is that which colours every page of the Prophecy, it is that which lifts his words from the realms of poetry into the rarefied air of the highest mystical expression. Love alone fills and unites creation ; Love alone explains the mystery of suffering ; it is Love that links together God and man, heaven and earth, man and life ; Love is the beginning and end, the meaning of all. And it is the office of Love— Love as the only true wealth that man can possess —that Isaias is commissioned to teach.

When the Lord has accepted the Prophet's oblation, He tells him at once what sort of a reception he must expect : Isaias will find that he will not be listened to. The Prophet asks whether such a state of affairs is going to last the whole course of his ministry. ' Until the cities be wasted without inhabitant,' is the answer, ' and the houses without man and the land shall be left desolate.' So the Prophet gets little consolation out of that ! He is told to preach the word and show the vision . . . and all that will result will be the harden-ing of hearts and the blinding of eyes. *In*directly his work may have the most far-reaching results, but *out*wardly—and indeed in actual fact—it will only make things worse : the unheeded message will render all the more insensible the already dulled minds of his hearers. What a prospect for the would-be apostle ! But that is the way in which the prophets are entrusted with their missions : they must woo their flocks, even as the Lord has already wooed their own souls. It is by showing to the faithful how God, like a man who plays a fish to land, is ready to ' play ' His creatures into His embrace that the prophets have justified their purpose. And Isaias had reason to know—if anyone had—how the Lord had ' played ' his soul. But to his hearers, the Jews who understood the language of smoke, and creaking lintels, and burning coals, this doctrine of a God who could woo a race and woo a prophet was a very strange doctrine indeed ; it was, in fact, too much for them. They did not take it. But wait, the situation was not entirely unrelieved ; the last words of the chapter which describes Isaias's call are these : ' that which shall stand therein shall be a holy seed.' Always a remnant . . . always a seed. The least of all seeds—like that of the mustard tree. So Isaias had something to go upon after all ; in fact he had everything, for he had the care of God.

CHAPTER III

IN JOATHAM'S REIGN

i

WE have now to go back again to the beginning of the
Prophecy. The incident which we have looked at in
the foregoing chapter must have preceded the delivery
of the prophecies contained in Isaias i–v. Ch. vi, the
initiation chapter, was either written by the Prophet
later on, or else judged by him (or possibly even by a
subsequent editor) to come more fittingly at the end
instead of at the beginning of those chapters of which
it is the complement; certainly the early chapters of
the Prophecy give us the lie of the land as it was at
the close of Ozias's reign and during the first years of
Joatham's.

Thus if Ozias died almost immediately after Isaias's
vision the prophecies in ch. iv must have been delivered
between 740 and, roughly, 737, before the political
situation began to change in Joatham's reign. Joatham
seems to have been a good enough king, judging the
people wisely and keeping them out of mischief, but
his period on the throne is not an interesting one.
Joatham had been acting as king during the latter
part of his father's reign because, as we know from
4 Kings xv, Azarias (as he is called here) ' was a leper
until the day of his death, and he dwelt in a free house
apart.' Joatham seems to have escaped the evil which
had come upon his predecessor, though he is accused

of falling into the same sin. Azarias was afflicted with leprosy because he had not stamped out the idolatry of his people; Joatham, we are told, ' did that which was right before the Lord, but the high places he took not away: the people still sacrificed and. burned incense. . . .'

Joatham was lucky, because nothing very exciting happened to him during the course of his sixteen years of power. We are perhaps mildly surprised to find that Isaias was in Jerusalem all this time and that still nothing was done to exterminate false worship. With a tolerably right-minded young man upon the throne —' he was twenty-five when he began to reign '—one would have thought that some effort might have been made. Perhaps Isaias did his best to persuade the king to take steps but had too much opposition to encounter from those who stood to gain by the continuance of the evil; he is certainly very bitter against the corrupt ministers of his time. Perhaps one can see in the king's building activities an attempt, feeble enough in all conscience, to satisfy the Prophet's exhortations and to quiet the promptings of his own sense of duty: Joatham ' built the highest gate in the house of the Lord.' But that was about the only thing he did in the whole of his sixteen years! Let us hope that Joatham raised this gate of his in the true spirit of the love of God; his son's architectural ventures were embarked upon from very worldly motives; we shall deal with that in its proper place. It is only a pity that the well-meaning but half-hearted Joatham died when he did; if he had remained on the throne of Juda for another ten years it is possible that the passive policy which Isaias was advocating would have been accepted. Joatham would have been only too glad to have let things slide ; but with his death came Achaz upon the throne of Juda, and he was a wicked and a meddlesome person as we shall see.

ii

Ch. i of the Prophecy as it stands is clearly to be attributed to the 740–739 period, ch. ii–iv may possibly belong to 734–733, but as all five chapters deal with the same situation we shall heap them together under a single heading, thus bringing ourselves, at their conclusion, abreast of ch. vii.

The cue to these first chapters is given in the verse which follows the superscription. ' Hear, O ye heavens,' cries the Prophet by way of proclamation, ' and give ear, O earth, for the Lord hath spoken. I have brought up children and exalted them, but they have despised Me. The ox knoweth his owner and the ass his master's crib, but Israel hath not known Me and My people hath not understood.'

The burden of this discourse, as has been suggested above, is expressed in a reproach to the Jews for their tendency to make rash alliances. ' I have brought up children and exalted them ' is a reference to the peaceful times which the Jews had enjoyed under Ozias and which they were still enjoying under their new sovereign ; ' but they have despised Me ' : lulled to sleep in their prosperity the sons of Juda had forgotten to whom it was that they owed their security. Isaias tells them that it is high time that they returned thanks. In neglecting to acknowledge Divine protection the Jews were as good as throwing off that protection altogether . . . which meant that they would be completely without protection, because they were certainly not able to hold their own against the enemy nations round about. If virtue, and wisdom, and safety lay in clinging on to God with both hands, then it was sin, and folly, and peril to repudiate—either designedly or in their way of living—that same protective Lord. ' They have forsaken the Lord . . . they have gone away backwards . . . the whole head is sick, the whole heart is sad.' Having failed in the one purpose of their being they are naturally ' sick ' and ' sad.'

Now the Prophet's hearers must have been thoroughly shaken by this ; it was news to them. It is always more exasperating to be told the truth about oneself when one has not the answer ready—especially when one has never dreamt of an answer being needed ! The easy-going Jews, in imitation of their sovereign lord and king, imagined that they were sufficiently law-abiding to escape prophetical censure : their Temple services, for example, were being carried out with some ceremony, their priests were numerous, their sacrifices were fat, the full ritual was being maintained, their alms . . . ' Your *what* ? ' cries Isaias ; ' who wants alms and ceremonial observances from people whose hearts are in the condition that yours are in ? ' Listen to the actual words of the Prophet, they are a perfect sermon on the subject of skin-deep piety :

' Hear the word of the Lord, ye rulers of Sodom ; give ear to the voice of our God, ye people of Gomorrha. To what purpose do you offer Me the multitude of your victims, saith the Lord ? I am full, I desire not holocausts of rams, and fat of fatlings, and blood of calves and lambs and buck-goats. When you came before Me, who required these things at

your hands, that you should walk in My courts?
Offer sacrifice now no more in vain; incense is an
abomination to Me. The new moons and the sabbaths
and the other festivals I will not abide; your assemblies
are wicked. My soul hateth your new moons and your
solemnities, they are become troublesome to me. I
am weary of bearing them. And when you stretch
forth your hands I will turn away My eyes from you;
and when you multiply prayer I will not hear. For
your hands are full of blood. Wash yourselves, be
clean. Take away the evil of your devices from My
eyes. Cease to do perversely. Learn to do well. Seek
judgement. Relieve the oppressed. Judge the father-
less. Defend the widow. And then come and accuse
Me, saith the Lord.' This is a passage that has helped
many a succeeding prophet!

Hard as he is on the lifeless worship which he detects
in the religiosity of Juda, Isaias gives his hearers a
chance. He says they can still *learn* to 'do well,'
'seek judgement,' and the rest; the door is not closed
to God's Mercy; in fact the next verse after the above
is an appeal in the tenderest terms to penance and a
return to the Lord. 'If your sins be as scarlet they
shall be made as white as snow; and if they be red
as crimson they shall be made white as wool.' Is this
listened to? Not at all! Or rather, not at all by the
majority but very earnestly by that faithful seed, that
little group of generous souls who, thank God, are in
every congregation however obstinate. And it will
be this mere handful—so inconsiderable a body as
hardly to be included in the Juda to which the Prophet
preached, so unrepresentative a faction that Isaias
could still point to the '*whole* head' that it was sick,
and the '*whole* heart' that it was sad—that must

merit to be called 'the faithful city.' There will be purgings and tribulations, but 'Sion shall be redeemed in judgement, and they shall bring her back in peace.'

So much for Isaias's first spoken discourse. He has established himself as a reformer. Like Amos in Israel, Isaias directs in Juda the God-sent attack upon the great; it is the rulers, the judges, and the priests that are the men responsible for the apostasy. They have so dragged down the nation as a whole that the nation as a whole must suffer; it is not now a case of the innocent with the guilty, it is a case of everyone being guilty. Did I say *everyone*? ' (reflects the Prophet); ' well, *nearly* everyone . . .' and then, as so often in the book of this idealist Prophet, the apostle in the man seems to break loose and, forgetting the sternness of his message, the gentle Prophet is carried away by the thought of what this 'remnant' will effect.

We can see Isaias going home on the evening of his sermon. He has often made speeches in public, but he has never done anything quite like this before. Proud of his achievement? Hardly, because after all he has probably achieved nothing but unpopularity and cheap notoriety. No, Isaias is certainly not *proud* of his day's work—not from the human point of view at all events—he is probably much more mystified, wondering at the grace that has been moving his lips and stirring his soul. Or perhaps he is so absorbed in the thought of the future that there is no room in his mind for speculation about the immediate past . . . he is dreaming of the new community, the social order which will one day come into being (and which will be described for us in the Acts of the Apostles), the ideal commonwealth as planned by God . . . grouping itself round the Ideal Man, God's Son. Isaias

sees more clearly than any other prophet (pardon me
this oft-repeated phrase) the need of the State to rest
on the grace of God alone ; in the Juda of his time he
sees a nation that is kept together by the vested
interests of man. Isaias is the first to conceive of an
ideal socialism, that *civitas Dei* which, like a lodestone,
is to draw him through the labyrinth of his many
chapters and his many disappointments. As I said
at the beginning, Isaias is the Gospel's pre-evangelist.

iii

Take now the second discourse—all that falls within
ch. ii–v and which belongs, as we have suggested, to
the same reign—and see how the Prophet's self-
confidence is asserting itself (the effect, if such a
distinction need be made, of confidence in God).
Reader, I am afraid I must admit that the above remark
was made in the hope that you would read the chapters
for yourself ; because it is here that we shall have to
make a rapid survey of contemporary politics in order
to get some idea of what is behind the Prophet's words
in these and the succeeding prophecies. At least let
it be said that I pay my reader the compliment of
letting him find out something for himself ; in fact
I could not be more rewarded than that he should
find out more than I have done ; which, if he be
fortunate enough to know Hebrew, he must infallibly
do. I was talking to a certain leader of Catholic
apologetics a few days ago, and learned to my dismay
that I was living without, and was likely to go on
living without, a sovereign remedy against depression.
However remote would appear to him the conversion
of England, and however dull a face his public

would turn towards him, Isaias in the Hebrew—and especially the ' second ' Isaias—was able, nearly always, to restore his good spirits within the hour. Those of us who have not the Hebrew tongue labour, it seems, under one of life's major disadvantages. . . . Courage, reader, courage ! It may be that you will derive from the English what my friend derives from the Hebrew ; even as it is printed in our own language I am prepared to claim for the Prophecy of Isaias that it ranks high among the finest pieces of literature in the world.

If ch. i was by way of introduction, ch. ii–v give us the kind of thing we are to expect throughout the Prophecy. But because the writer is here still rather general in his application, these addresses cannot with certainty be pinned down to a definite date. The state of the country during the latter part of Joatham's reign, however, will be given here, and it will be seen how far the present chapters are relevant.

We have already noted that Juda had, for generations past, enjoyed an almost miraculous immunity from any kind of large-scale invasion. The same had been the case of the sister-nation, Israel. It is true that Juda and Israel had carried on a sort of guerrilla warfare between themselves, and there had been lively encounters with Philistia from time to time, but until the eighth century B.C. there was no question of either nation being swamped by a really great power. This happy state of affairs was only in danger of being altered when a number of remarkable men followed one another on the throne of Assyria. The rise of Nineveh, Assyria's capital, marks the change of fortune for Israel (that is to say, Israel *and* Juda, the two nations are called by the name of the senior). The colonization of Assyria in the century we are consider-

ing reads like a fable ; Nineveh's advance in arms,
culture, science, and politics can hardly be equalled
in the history of the human race. It was for Isaias and
his fellow-prophets to warn the Chosen People of the
Assyrian menace ; and, having warned them, to warn
them what *not* to do to meet it.

The first of these great Assyrian kings was Theglathphalasar III, who reigned from 745 B.C. till 727 ;
these dates are fixed for us by Assyrian monuments,
showing that the period covered by the reign coincides
roughly with the beginning of Isaias's ministry at the
court of Ozias and the end of Achaz's reign when the
Prophet was the fully recognized mouthpiece of God.
Theglathphalasar, who comes in the Book of Kings
(IV, xv), seems to have had all the military genius of
the greatest of the Romans, of whom he only fell short
in the matter of home government and national
consolidation. He subdued in his time the people of
Syria, Babylonia, Gaza (in Philistia), and Hamath.
He appointed himself king over Babylonia.

It is significant to note that the enemy nation of
which Theglathphalasar was king, first interested itself
in the affairs of the Chosen People at the invitation of
the Chosen People themselves ; not, perhaps, at the
invitation of the majority, but certainly at the invitation of the most influential in the realm—headed by
the king. And this is the way it came about :

The little kingdom of Hamath (mentioned above at
the end of the list of Assyria's conquests—and mentioned rather in a whisper because the overthrow of
Hamath would hardly have ranked with the other of
Theglathphalasar's triumphs) had been allied with Juda
in bonds of mutual agreement for a very long time—
since the days of King David in fact. Each nation found

a common enemy in Syria. Now when the Assyrian emperor annexed Hamath, Juda was in the unfortunate position of being exposed to Syria on the east. True, Syria was not as powerful as it had been (and was soon to suffer a complete eclipse), but from other sides also the borders of Juda were insecure : was not Assyria sweeping down from the north and north-east ? Had not Egypt freedom of access from the south ?

Egypt had given no trouble up to date, and there was no particular reason to believe that its intentions were hostile now, but this people was, with Babylonia, the third giant nation of the Near East, and, should it become a matter of war between Assyria and Egypt, Juda's position on the map might make it very difficult for her not to become the battle-ground. The odd part of it is that nobody seems to have seen the danger until Isaias pointed it out. We shall watch him point it out when we come to deal with the measures he took to prevent disaster ; at this early stage he is still trying to convince his hearers that they are deserving of some really severe punishment at the hand of God. This done, it will be time for the Prophet to draw attention to two points : first, what had looked like an effete civilization twenty years ago (Assyria) was showing every sign of being master of Palestine to-day ; and second, what had looked like a world power twenty years ago was now nothing but a bundle of splendid records and empty boasts (Egypt). But the pointing out of these facts, together with an account of the part played by Syria in the matter, we can delay for consideration until Isaias's spade-work has been examined. The Prophet prepares the ground as follows :

Opening his discourse with a statement as to the
glittering benefits with which he sees his Juda blessed,
' their land is filled,' says Isaias (and indeed Juda was
better off than it had been since Solomon's day, and
better off certainly than was the sister-nation Israel),
' with silver and gold, and there is no end of their
treasures ; and their land is filled with horses, and their
chariots are innumerable ' ; in other words, Juda
wants for nothing . . . not even false worship, for ' their
land is also full of idols.' During Isaias's lifetime
Jerusalem had been becoming more and more a centre
of smartness, wealth, luxury, and doubtful commerce ;
its geographical position had assisted this, Jerusalem
lying as it did on a trade-route which was very much
used at that time. Buffer states enjoy privileges
besides enduring dangers : you cannot have it both
ways.

We can imagine the Prophet getting up on to a
platform in one of the outer courts of the Temple and
delivering his address to a mixed assembly. It is
probably a feast-day, and he starts on a note of general
congratulation : a glowing tribute is made to the
nation's good fortune. And then, quite suddenly,
comes the bombshell : ' The land is full of idols.'
The Prophet then proceeds to reveal the whole horror
of Juda's condition. Perhaps he had begun smiling
so that his frown might be all the more effective ; perhaps his smile had been put on in order to get the people
to listen at all ; perhaps, even, he had smiled sar-
castically (but I do not think that this was it—Isaias
is not a cynic). At all events he is not smiling now.
' Therefore forgive them not.' Whatever it was at the
beginning, the sermon is scarcely developing along
festal lines. Even if Isaias, labouring at his preparation

overnight, had made ready a panegyric for his hearers
he is certainly forced now by the Spirit to pronounce
a doom instead.

As a matter of fact this last suggestion is not
improbable when we consider the congregation he is
speaking to. Many a preacher who mounts the pulpit
with the best will in the world is found to change his
plans. I know a Friar Preacher whose sad experience
it is that whenever he determines to call his audience
to the heights of sanctity he is driven, when watching
the effect of his words, to alter his tone and to beg
that his hearers may resolve to avoid the occasions of
mortal sin.

Well, for about twenty-five verses the Prophet
pitches into the Jews for their sins : he tells them what
will be the outcome of all this idolatry : they will have
to face poverty, subjection, panic. They will be hood-
winked by their adversaries, they will be wasted by
disease. And then, just when you are thinking that
the mild Isaias has shown about as much of his tongue
as will convince the Jews of the roughness of its edge,
he really lashes out ! See how he descends from the
general to the particular—from ' The Lord will enter
into judgement with the ancients of His people ' to,
two verses later, ' The daughters of Sion are haughty,
and have walked with stretched-out necks and wanton
glances of their eyes, and made a noise as they walked
with their feet. . . .' It looks as if the Prophet's eye
has been caught, while he is in the full flood of his
sermon, by the distracting behaviour of one of these
very ' daughters of Sion.' Listen to the rest of the
passage and tell me if you do not agree :

' The Lord will make bald the crown of the head of
the daughters of Sion ; and the Lord will discover their

hair.' ['Discover'—I ask you! could a better word
be found for the process in the whole of the English
language? The idea suggested being a mixture of
'taking off the cover' and 'revealing the poverty
underneath.' No, I would not exchange the English
for the Hebrew in spite of what has been said above.
Even our text has gloom-relieving properties.] 'In
that day the Lord will take away the ornaments of
shoes, and little moons; and chains, and necklaces,
and bracelets, and bonnets, and bodkins, and ornaments of the legs, and tablets, and sweet balls, and
ear-rings, and rings, and jewels hanging on the forehead, and changes of apparel, and short cloaks, and
fine linen and crisping-pins; and looking-glasses, and
lawns, and head-bands, and fine veils. And instead of
a sweet smell there shall be a stench; and instead of
a girdle a cord. And instead of curled hair, baldness;
and instead of a stomacher, haircloth. Thy fairest
men also shall fall by the sword; and thy valiant
ones in battle. And her gates shall lament and mourn;
and she shall sit desolate on the ground.' And with
that the chapter closes. Whether it was the end of the
discourse or not we do not know—probably not—but
it was the end of the illuminating little digression on
the 'modern young woman.'

Even if we had not the above-quoted passage to
show us what class of person Isaias was addressing we
know from his earlier references in the same sermon to
'judges,' 'councillors,' 'captains over fifty,' and
'architects' that his congregation was mostly drawn
from the upper strata of Jerusalem society. He knows
exactly the kinds of lives these people are leading, he
has lived in that world himself: nothing but money,
money, money, and all the pleasures that money

alone can provide. Isaias speaks of the Lord ' entering into judgement with His princes,' but it is not only with the blood royal that the Lord finds reason to be angry—the ' captains of fifty ' are every bit as much to blame (we think of these military gentlemen shifting uneasily in their places—they are conspicuous in their uniforms—and wishing more earnestly than usual that the sermon will be a short one) . . . so are ' the skilful in eloquent speech' every bit as much to blame, politicians who have twisted the masses round their little fingers with cant phrases and specious reasonings . . . *these* are the men who will see the tables turned. They have trusted in diplomacy, have they? In wealth, position, power ? Well, they will admit one day that it would have been better had they had trusted in God. And then at this point some silly simpering woman (I may be wrong about this) makes her way—which is an elaborate one—to the sort of pen where the Hebrew ladies are enclosed. When she has settled herself the chattering, and the giggling, and the ogling break out again—interrupted only by the Prophet's eloquence or the lady's insolence—and Isaias, who has been a little bit distracted all along by this section of his audience, becomes frankly exasperated.

If there was a burble of voices at the beginning of his sermon we can be fairly sure that there is silence at the close. We do not need much imagination to see how the ' daughters of Sion ' take their leave : not a sound from a single loose-heeled shoe ! Painted and jewelled hands are clasping the tell-tale bracelets and necklaces, muffling and hiding them as far as the ' short cloaks ' will allow. The ornaments, too, and the ' little moons ' are deftly veiled by the ' fine linen ' to which the Prophet has taken such exception. But the

D

Prophet, standing in the shade of the Temple's porch, sees it all . . . he sees the sun on the pins which adorn the hair ; he sees the gold and the glass which is *not* covered up . . . jewels that hang on a forehead here and an ankle there. . . . Ugh ! And worst of all are the charms, the emblems of false belief—those more than ' fashionable little vanities ' which are symptomatic of the people's creeds. Perhaps (and I hope we can lay claim to some such fancy) a few of those who came late, as to an entertainment, stayed late in the Temple for purposes of prayer. It would be doing an injustice to the people of the Holy City—and it would not be very flattering to the Prophet—if we were to take it for granted that not a single 'strong, cunning, and ancient man ' was touched by the words he had heard, and that not a single ' haughty ' maid had been brought to her knees in prayer.

If the chapter which separates the foregoing from the famous ' vineyard ' chapter is still part of the same discourse, as indeed seems likely, then the change back again from the particular to the general, from the immediate to the future, is most marked. And, as always happens when Isaias has been upbraiding his flock and is coming to the end of his address, the condemnation turns into a last-moment reprieve—at all events for the ' few.' ' And you will live happily ever afterwards, *but*, my friends, at a cost.' With the result that the Prophet's hearers go home that day having several clear-cut thoughts to digest in the privacy of their drawing-rooms : first, they must know that their prosperity comes from God and no one else ; second, that this prosperity has been used all wrong ; and third, that God will renew His protec-tion when the price has once been paid . . . but His

protection will not show itself on the old lines of
material well-being. . . . 'Every one that shall be left
shall be called holy.' 'Holy,' not 'prosperous.' In
spiritual abundance shall the New Jerusalem be
founded; 'a cloud by day and a smoke and the
brightness of a flaming fire in the night'—such as
their ancestors had known in the wilderness—shall be
their security . . . supernatural defences are to take
the place of the 'high towers' and 'fenced walls' in
which they glory now.

iv

Isaias's next address is The Reproach of the Vineyard, which is one of the most moving appeals in the
whole of the Bible. It would make this little book of
mine exceedingly complicated if we were to chop up
the Prophet's sixty-six chapters into separate sermons,
so I shall confine myself to picking out what I consider
to be the richest passages in Isaias and delivering little
sermons of my own. The reader who trembles before
this proposal (or who, by the law of association,
yawns) can cheer himself with the thought that there
will, of necessity, be a certain amount of history into
which he can get his teeth, and that most of the
moralizing will be by the way.

' I will sing to my beloved the canticle of my cousin
concerning his vineyard. My beloved had a vineyard
on a hill in a fruitful place. And he fenced it in and
picked the stones out of it, and planted it with the
choicest vines, and built a tower in the midst thereof, and
set up a winepress therein. And he looked that it should
bring forth grapes, and it brought forth wild grapes.
And now, O ye inhabitants of Jerusalem and ye men

of Juda, judge between me and my vineyard. What
is there that I ought to do more to my vineyard that
I have not done to it ? Was it that I looked that it
should bring forth grapes and it hath brought forth
wild grapes ? And now I will show you what I will do
to my vineyard. I will take away the hedge thereof
and it shall be wasted ; I will break down the wall
thereof and it shall be trodden down. And I will make
it desolate. It shall not be pruned and it shall not be
digged ; but briers and thorns shall come up. And I
will command the clouds to rain no more upon it.
For the vineyard of the Lord of Hosts is the house of
Israel.'

What a parable ! And not a wasted word. The
Church does well to select verses from this passage
for her Good Friday liturgy. The reproach cuts deep.

Notice how, by the end of it, the Prophet has forgotten about his ' cousin,' it is now ' the Lord of
Hosts ' who is the owner of the barren property.
Surely Our Lord—and Our Lord's hearers—must have
been thinking of this chapter in Isaias when He spoke
of the fig-tree planted in a vineyard : ' and he came
seeking fruit on it and he found none ' . . . and again,
seven chapters later in the same S. Luke, when he
told how the lord of the vineyard ' will come and
destroy these husbandmen, and will give the vineyard
to others. . . . Which they hearing, said to Him :
God forbid ' ? The moral is the same : infidelity—
consistent infidelity and not a mere now-and-then
lapse—wrests away the choicest gifts . . . which we,
knowing, say : ' God forbid.' In presuming to call
Isaias the ' Man of Ideas ' I have always thought that
this idea of the vineyard was one of his finest. It is
possible that Jeremias was of the same opinion, because

an echo of Isaias's voice is surely to be heard in the
later prophet's more stinging words : ' Many pastors
have destroyed my vineyard, they have trodden my
portion under foot, they have turned my delightful
portion into a desolate wilderness. They have laid it
waste and it hath mourned for me. With desolation
is all the land made desolate, because there is none
that considereth in the heart.' But perhaps after all
I am doing Jeremias an injury ; the poignant sorrow
of the words is so typical of the man of tears that
perhaps he seized upon the most desolate of all things
—a garden run to waste—entirely on his own.

To go back to the vineyard of Isaias, what more
could the Beloved have done for it ? What more—
carrying the parable down to our own day—*can* the
Beloved do for *us* ? With the Gospel in our hands and
the Blessed Sacrament on our altars there is nothing
more the Beloved can do. He has shed His last drop
of Blood for His vineyard. Surely it is not fanciful to
say that He has ' fenced us in ' with the protection of
His grace—we are safe here, unless we break down the
barriers ourselves—that He has ' picked out the stones '
from us by the Sacraments of Baptism and Confession,
that He has ' planted the choicest vines ' in us by the
gifts of the Holy Spirit ? Are we not, also, ' set on a
hill '—like the City to which Our Lord referred ?
Have we not a ' tower ' in which to shelter—one
founded upon a rock ? Have we not winepresses, too,
in every country where Christ is preached ? At times
it happens that blood is mingled with the flow of wine,
but even if persecution is absent from our ' fruitful '
land, the treading out the grape must still go on : we
energize—' pruning ' and ' digging ' in the vineyard—
for our fellow-men. What else is Catholic Action but a

winepress within a tower ? ' Judge between Me and
My vineyard. . . . I looked that it should bring forth
grapes . . . and it brought forth wild grapes.' Wild,
independently grown, bitter-tasting-and-shrivelled-up
grapes. . . . Oh God, let us cling to the True Vine !

But the sermon of the vineyard is not finished. While
their iniquity is still before their eyes and they are yet
tingling with shame, Isaias, who is nothing if not
opportunist in his dealings with repentant nations and
repentant kings, lashes out with stroke upon stroke,
showing to his audience each separate evil of which
it stands guilty in the sight of God. He tells the rich
merchants how displeasing to the Lord are the ' great
and fair houses ' (and the Prophet waves his hand in
the direction of the rich residential quarter ; the roofs
of the greater dwellings can be seen from the Temple
terrace). What is wrong, do they ask, in possessing a
house and lands ? ' I will tell,' says Isaias, ' what is
wrong ! It is sin to "lay field to field " by shifty
contracts ; it is sin to extort taxes from such as are
powerless to pay ; it is sin to profit by labour that is
sweated . . . *and these things are in my ears*, saith the
Lord of Hosts.' Isaias touches, briefly but very
sharply, on drunkenness, on the self-satisfaction of the
' wise ', on the corruption that exists in high places . . .
small wonder, implies the Prophet, that Juda is rotten
to the core : sleek and beautiful on the outside but
rotten, rotten, rotten, is the nation within. What is
God going to do about it ? This will He do : ' He will
lift up a sign to the nations afar off, and will whistle
to them from the ends of the earth, and behold they
will come with speed swiftly. . . .' Assyria, Chaldea,
and finally Persia, so many tools of vengeance summon-
ed to strike the Chosen People by the common Lord of

all mankind Who can ' whistle ' for whom He will,
' and behold they will come with speed swiftly . . .
their arrows are sharp, and all their bows are bent ;
the hoofs of their horses shall be like the flint, and their
wheels like the violence of the tempest . . . we
shall look towards the land [' we,' notice, not the
reprobate only, but ' we '—all of us] and behold
darkness of tribulation : and the light is darkened
with the mist thereof.' Which is the end of Isaias's
recorded words as preached in the reign of Joatham,
king of Juda. We are now, having dealt with ch. vi
in the beginning, abreast of the important section
which deals with the Prophet's activities in Achaz's
time. The political situation outlined in this chapter
will soon be coming to a head.

' The light is darkened with the mist thereof.' Ah,
yes, there would be more of darkness than of light in
the reign that was to follow . . . and if there is one thing
more depressing than a wasted vineyard it is seeing in
the mists of twilight a scene that has been loved in the
sun.

CHAPTER IV

IN ACHAZ'S REIGN

i

ANOTHER brief historical survey is necessary here if we would form an estimate of the Prophet's influence on the happenings of this reign. We have left Theglath-phalasar subduing Hamath and threatening to subdue the rest of Palestine. By the time that Achaz had succeeded to the throne, the whole of northern Galilee had fallen before the Assyrian hordes, and the tribe of Nephtali had been carried off captive (4 Kings xv, 29). Things were beginning to look serious for Juda ; the new king must have been cursing the day his father died. 'Achaz was twenty years old when he began to reign, and he reigned sixteen years in Jeru-salem,' and the Book of Kings goes on to say—but we could have guessed as much from the Prophecy of Isaias—that 'he did not that which was pleasing in the sight of the Lord his God, as David his father, but he walked in the ways of the kings of Israel.' Juda's immediate neighbours, Syria and Samaria, have hardly been mentioned as yet because we have considered only the greater powers that were menacing Jerusalem at the time, but it was these two, relatively smaller, nations that were to cause the disturbances which agitated the reign of Achaz.

Syria and Samaria had for some time been paying tribute to Assyria but had entered into a pact together with a view to throwing off the yoke. Feeling, however, that by themselves they would be hopelessly outnumbered they entered tentatively into negotiations with Juda's king. This must have happened almost as soon as Achaz ascended the throne (734), because we read in the account of the Book of Kings already referred to that ' Rasin king of Syria, and Phacee son of Romelia king of Israel, came up to Jerusalem to fight. And they besieged Achaz but were not able to overcome him.' The same is borne out by Isaias, who says further (vii, 1) that though they ' could not prevail over Jerusalem ' they managed to have a very frightening effect upon that city and upon its king : ' and his heart was moved and the heart of his people, as the trees of the woods are moved with the wind.'

It is not hard to find a reason for the complete change of policy as revealed in the sudden aggression on the part of Syria and Samaria. What had happened was this : Achaz had turned down the overtures of the two neighbouring chieftains, Rasin and Phacee, because he was much more afraid of Assyria than he was of people whom his race had been fighting in a desultory way for generations. He knew that if Juda were pledged to the revolt, then nothing would ever save him from the wrath of Theglathphalasar if once that mighty man came out victorious. On the other hand, if the revolt should prove successful without his co-operation he stood rather to gain than to lose . . . and if it failed, well, Juda would not be mixed up in it. But this did not suit the plans of Rasin and Phacee who at all costs wanted men, money, and horses. So they tried to dethrone Achaz and put on Tabeel in his place ; this is the ' fight ' referred to in Isaias and the Book of Kings. The thing was an outrage to the

Jewish nation because Tabeel was a stranger and an
alien, more of an unbeliever than anything to be
found in Samaria—which after all was part of Israel.[1]
Rasin and Phacee had every reason to be desperate
(as events subsequently showed when their revolt was
stamped out incontinently), and if they were unable
either to entice Achaz to join them or to force the
nation's hand, at least they could terrorize the people
of Jerusalem and hope for the best in the way of
deserters. Achaz was beginning badly. Here was
Assyria looking uglier and uglier ; here were these two
king-makers harrying his borders whenever they got
the chance ; and, most ominous of all, here was a
division of opinion in Jerusalem. Achaz, though a
weak man as we shall see, seems to have been con-
sistently pro-Assyrian throughout, but he must have
found it hard to keep this up in the face of the opposite
sympathies which were showing themselves in his
capital.   In the end, after temporizing for some
years, Achaz threw in his lot with Nineveh—Assyria's
capital and Theglathphalasar's stronghold—asking in
return for tribute the support and protection of the
unbeliever against the common enemies, Syria and
Samaria.

This staved off the Assyrian invasion which had been
so much dreaded in the previous reign, but it also had
the effect of making Egypt restive in the south. With
Juda's Egyptian policy, however, we shall deal on a
later page. The curtain goes up on King Achaz after
a year or two of power (Isaias is that rather sinister
figure behind the throne).

[1] Originally, and even up to the time of David, the kingdom of
Syria had been part of the kingdom of Israel. In Solomon's time
the Syrian monarchy was founded, and Damascus became the capital
of the first Syrian king, Rasin.

ii

' And the Lord said to Isaias : Go forth to meet
Achaz, thou and Jasub thy son that is left, to the
conduit of the upper pool, in the way of the fuller's
field.'

We read this and we say : ' Ah, the Lord is going
to dictate Juda's policy after all. Splendid ! There
will probably be instructions about some sort of
compromise with Rasin and Phacee ; anything in
preference to alliance with the unbelieving Assyrian.'
We find ourselves instinctively thinking along the lines
of the people of Jerusalem : the less fighting to be
done the better, and let's hope that we won't have the
heathen for an ally.[1] But if these are our views they
are not the views of the Lord as interpreted by Isaias.
The Prophet mistrusted the All-Israel-cum-Syria coali-
tion as much as he feared the threatening Assyrian.
He saw in the man Tabeel (Rasin's and Phacee's
candidate for the throne of Juda) a Syrian domination
no less destructive of Juda's integrity than what he
saw in the man Theglathphalasar. Isaias was for
neither allegiance ; Isaias was for national independence. His programme was one which might well
make the most daring of foreign secretaries gasp :
' leave them alone and trust in God.' And yet, when
we look a little more deeply into the matter, the line
which the Prophet adopted was the only one consistent
with what he knew to be his and his country's vocation.
He would have been hard put to it, in other words, to
countenance a league that was plotting against the

[1] Because though generations had passed since Syria had split
off, it was still regarded as less of a pagan kingdom than the
Assyrian.

House of David—however impossible was its scion—
while he would have been equally averse to submission
to a nation that threatened the religious life of Juda.
So Isaias held out boldly for the unpopular and
unromantic—but godly—course of wait-and-see.

Thus you have the following thoughts running
through the Prophet's mind as he makes his way, with
little Jasub's hand in his, towards the ' conduit of the
upper pool ' : first, the king's sympathies are obviously
in the Assyrian direction (so much so that he has
probably pledged himself already) ; second, the people
of Jerusalem, demoralized by the proximity of the
Syrian forces and the memory of such incursions as
Juda has suffered in the previous reign from the
Samaritans, are mostly pro-Rasin ; third, Achaz is a
weak man, inheriting all his father's shortcomings and
adding a measure of godlessness all his own. What is
Isaias's message to the king, the policy which the
Lord will have Israel to follow ?

' And thou shalt say to him '—so run the instructions
of God—' See thou be quiet ; fear not and let not thy
heart be afraid of the two tails of these firebrands,
smoking with the wrath of the fury of Rasin king of
Syria, and of the son of Romelia.' All of which, and
a good deal more, does Isaias pass on to the king of
Juda.

It is a strange scene that is presented to us : an
intimate parley between a very downright prophet and
a very hesitating prince. The fact that it takes
place where it does—at the conduit—is significant :
Achaz, obviously in a panic over the defences of his
city, has gone to the ' upper pool ' in order to make
sure that Jerusalem will be well supplied with water
in the event of a siege. Here, at a place which is called

the Virgin's Spring (and where, in Ezechias's reign, another important event is to take place), Isaias confronts his sovereign with a word on his lips from the Lord. The sun is high in the heavens . . . the city is spread out before them, for they are on elevated ground . . . there is the faint sound of flowing water . . . the little boy Jasub is fishing about in the shallows of the ' upper pool ' for tadpoles . . . the figures of the two men are outlined against the sky.

' See thou be quiet. . . . Rasin and Phacee are nothing but firebrands, adventurers carrying no weight whatever.' Isaias not only dismisses the two chieftains with a wave of the hand but goes on to prophesy the fate of the peoples they govern. ' The head of Syria is Damascus, and the head of Damascus is Rasin, and within threescore and five years, Ephraim shall cease to be a people ; and the head of Ephraim is Samaria, and the head of Samaria is the son of Romelia. [Here the Prophet seems to see the doubt that is working in the mind of his hearer, for he goes on :] If you will not believe you will not continue.'

This is no empty threat ; Damascus fell two years later (732) and ten years saw the finish of Samaria (722). Achaz has nothing to say, he merely looks exceedingly sceptical.

One can understand the feelings of the king ; he knows that if he accepts the Prophet's advice he will have to readjust his whole outlook. Achaz knows that he is not the man to restore the confidence of the people of Jerusalem, persuading them that there is nothing in this Syria-Ephraim business—that Rasin and his friends are calling a bluff. Achaz is as powerless to steady the nerves of Jerusalem as he is to steady his own . . . ' his heart was moved and the heart of his

people, as the trees of the woods are moved with the
wind.' Not used to trusting in the advice of his friends
he cannot bring himself to believe in the wisdom of the
man of God ; not used to acts of faith he cannot trust
in God Himself. As he stands there in the sunshine
he is desperately trying to make certain which nation
it is that is likely to be strongest in the field. In the
pause in the conversation Achaz surveys the surrounding country : whence help ? whence war ? . . . And it
seems to him that Nineveh, sinful, go-ahead, rich,
relentless Nineveh offers the best returns for Juda's
gold. Yes, he will plead for the hand of Nineveh . . .
but he will not mention the fact to the man who stands
before him on the hill.

Is it so very wrong of Achaz (perhaps you ask) to
curry favour with the strongest power ? Is it not a
king's business to do that sort of thing ? I suppose
Isaias would have answered that the king ought to
have known that Assyria was the strongest power *but
One*, and that those who curry favour must assess the
price of the currying. Has Achaz considered, for
example, the bleeding of his country dry under the
tax of Theglathphalasar ? The Chosen People to
become enslaved, depopulated, transported to other
lands . . . their precious inheritance—the faith—to be
exposed to the chill of scepticism. . . . ' If you will not
believe, you shall not continue.' Isaias knows, if the
king does not, the consequences of a heathen alliance.
And so the moments pass. With the finish of Isaias's
flow of words, Jasub, wondering what is going to happen
next, draws near to the two men and starts rolling
himself up in his father's flapping *talith ;* he has
finished his muddy game and is conscious that he is in
the middle of a ' situation.' The Prophet waits for his

sovereign's reply. Achaz, resenting Isaias's inter-
ference and hating thus to be forced into an admission
or a denial of God's Providence (for that is what it
comes to after all), clings to his silence.

'And the Lord spoke again to Achaz saying: Ask
thee a sign of the Lord thy God, either unto the depth
of hell, or unto the height above.' God is generous,
He offers to strengthen the king's confidence with any
miracle the king might fancy. 'And Achaz said: I
will not ask, I will not tempt the Lord.' O feeble
excuse! Like so many of us, my dear Achaz, you fear
the conviction which a sign will bring. Which means,
of course, that you *need* no sign—you are quite convinced already. Achaz, you are a hypocrite.

But Isaias is not to be put off. Going straight on
as though the king has not refused the offer, 'Hear
ye therefore, O house of David,' he says. 'Is it a
small thing for you to be grievous to men, that you
are grievous to my God also? Therefore the Lord
Himself shall give you a sign. BEHOLD A VIRGIN
SHALL CONCEIVE AND BEAR A SON, AND HIS NAME
SHALL BE CALLED EMMANUEL. He shall eat butter
and honey, that he may know to refuse the evil and
to choose the good.' It is hardly necessary to say that
the application of this prophecy to Our Lord has been
disputed, by Jews and Christians alike, so that it has
become one of those texts to which we can cling with
that glorious feeling that at all events we who are
within the Church know exactly Whom it is about!
It is not that the verse is a little private revelation to
those who believe a certain thing, it is much more that
a 'sign' is given us witnessing to the thing that we
believe. The 'sign' that Achaz rejected is given to
us instead.

The quantity of rubbish that has been written on the passage is truly astonishing ! The theory is advanced by one authority, for example, that the sign consists 'simply in the name which mothers will before long, by a kind of inspiration, give to their newly born babies'—Isaias being presumably used by the Lord to say what will become fashionable ! The words of v. 15, again (' He shall eat butter and honey, etc.'), are described as a ' misleading gloss.'

Briefly—very briefly—the reasons brought against the Messianic application of the prophecy are :

(i) That ' the sign ' was intended for Achaz's enlightenment, not for ours. To which we would answer that it was expressly given to ' the House of David '—continuing to the birth of Christ. Let Achaz believe and act upon it ; he will be rewarded, and his successors will see the fulfilment ; the two facts will bear each other out. But Achaz does not believe. The one fact, however, remains to bear witness to the truth of the Prophet's words : the fact of the miraculous birth of Christ.

(ii) That the sign referred to release from the Captivity. To which we say : ' Yes, from the captivity of darkness and in the Person of the true Light, Jesus Christ.'

(iii) That the Hebrew word which we translate as ' Virgin ' means nothing more than ' young woman.' (The words ' or maiden ' have been added in the Revised Version.) The only answer we would bring to this objection is that if virginity is not implied by the Prophet then there does not seem to be much of a ' sign ' in what he has to say.

(iv) That the application of the passage is to Isaias's second son. But we have seen that the name of the

Prophet's son was something quite different, and even if the child had possessed many names (as is more than possible), the 'child' spoken of here, the 'Emmanuel,' is evidently not as other children—apart altogether from the circumstances of his birth—for he shall be ' the owner of the land.'[1] Read Isaias's eighth and ninth chapters where he refers to this Emmanuel, and see if it is merely the boasting of a happy father. Further, if we have been right in thinking that the Prophet came of noble, or at any rate wealthy, stock then how should his child come to be nourished on 'butter and honey'—the food, apparently, of the very poor ? That Isaias's sons were both *types* of the Messias we have already seen, and this may explain the slight confusion, but to show that Isaias's 'Emmanuel' is no more important person than Marshalalhabaz is to claim both too much and too little.

'Emmanuel': God with us. Names have always an importance in Isaias. And so the best of all his names must go to Christ. ' God with us ' . . . *Dominus nobiscum* . . . volumes might be written on the Holy Name. We are not surprised that the Church has given us this, of all God's names, to think about at Christmas. ' Emmanuel ' is a prayer, a hope, a blessing, a *fact*. God, Christ, the Eternal Word, *is* WITH US. He is not any longer ' over ' but *with* us . . . not ' beyond,' or ' above,' or ' looking-at-from-afar ' (albeit with infinite tenderness) but *with* us. *Et habitavit in nobis* we read in the last gospel of the Mass. *Dominus vobiscum* says the priest.

With the end of v. 15 (' that he may know to refuse the evil and to choose the good ') the sense changes,

[1] viii, 8 ; our version has ' he will fill the breadth of thy land.'

E

and the Prophet leaves the subject of the Messias for
the more immediate ' thing that will come to pass,'
namely the fate of the Syria-Samaria combine.   ' For
before the [a] child know to refuse the evil and to
choose the good, the land which thou abhorrest shall
be forsaken of the face of her two kings.   The Lord
shall bring upon thee and upon thy people, and upon the
house of thy father, days that have not come since
the time of the separation of Ephraim from Juda with
the king of the Assyrians.'   The first part of the above
quotation is taken to mean that Rasin and Phacee
will cease to rule by the time that it takes for an
infant, conceived to-day, to arrive at an age when he
knows what it is that he wants and can ask for it.
This may quite well refer to Isaias's own son, but the
point of the statement seems to be that two years will
see the end of the dreaded league ; which, as we have
said, turned out to be so.

The Prophet's legatine mission failed.   Achaz sighed
and went home to the palace with his mind made up.
Theglathphalasar was informed of Juda's trust in his
protection.   Isaias returned to the ' middle city ' with
little Jasub's hand in his . . . and with supremely
contemptuous thoughts in his mind regarding the
wisdom of princes.

iii

It is now, when Isaias has finished his description
of the interview with Achaz, that we hear of the birth
of the second son.   There is therefore not a complete
lack of sequence in Isaias ; after what has been said
above this is just the place where we should expect to
find the circumstances of the second child's birth :

' if an infant were begotten to-day, by the time he could discern, etc.'—Isaias is taking occasion of his own affairs. We have touched upon the Lord's command that he should ' take a great book, and write in it with a man's pen,' and we have seen how the name which is to be given to the child is one that heralds misfortune ; we can go straight on, therefore, to examine the words which the Lord addresses to Isaias (and to the people of Juda) and which are the outcome of this event.

' Forasmuch as this people hath cast away the waters of Siloe that go with silence, and hath rather taken Rasin and the son of Romelia, therefore the Lord will bring upon them the waters of the river strong and many, the king of the Assyrians, and all his glory ; and he shall come up over all his channels and shall overflow all his banks.'

So the Prophet's curse is not reserved for the king alone ! He tells the people of Jerusalem that they are every bit as much to blame in taking up the policy opposed to the king. The protection of the Lord may appear to be as slender and as insignificant as the little stream that flows from the pool of Siloe, but if they treat it as of no account the Euphrates (Theglath-phalasar) will flood them utterly. Isaias, we notice, is not only asking of the people—as he asked of their king—a change of policy, he is asking of them a change of life.

Thus the general import of this section of the prophecy (viii–xiii) can be summed up in the verse ' I will wait for the Lord.' Patience, Faith, Abandonment are virtues dear to the heart of Isaias ; whenever, in fact, he is not employed on some special mission or endeavouring to stamp out some special abuse the

Prophet always says the same thing : ' See thou be quiet ; fear not. . . .' Isaias is the forerunner of Père de Caussade.

But Isaias is not listened to.

The step which Achaz has taken is, from his point of view, entirely successful : Assyria is pitting her vast strength against Syria and Samaria. Juda is safe—for the time being. It is true that the price of this friendship with Theglathphalasar is costing, as Isaias said it would, so much in hard coin that the Temple as well as the palace is being spoiled of its furniture to meet the tax. It will be some years before Juda finds that the price of the Assyrian friendship is even more than she bargained for, that the heathen race will show signs—to use Isaias's simile—of ' overflowing the banks,' but this will not be until the next reign. ' Sufficient for the day,' says Achaz . . . and does his best to avoid meeting the Prophet.

To cut a long story short, Juda found herself, by 730, shortly after the fall of Damascus, in much the same boat as Syria : both nations were paying tribute to the same lord. What has Isaias got to say about this ? As a matter of fact he has a great deal to say about it—so much that there is no room for the least hint of an I-told-you-so—and always his doctrine is consistent : ' Be quiet ; fear not ; wait for the Lord.' Up to date his advice has not been taken ; very good ; he is told that Juda is still divided and that the influential party is all for casting off the yoke of Assyria . . . does not the Prophet agree ? He has been so emphatic about not yoking the country to an unbeliever a few years back, does he not think it is high time now to cast off that yoke ? True, he should have been listened to in the first place but . . . well, it is surely not too late to make amends . . . what does the Prophet suggest ?

Contrary to the king's expectation the Prophet suggests doing absolutely nothing. Once the initial blunder has been made the only course is, in Isaias's opinion, to abide by the situation that results. ' You may not go against your feudal lord without good reason ' is the line which the Prophet takes with the people of Jerusalem, ' and the only reason you can advance for your rebellion is that you regret having become his serf.' If Isaias is not being as romantic and as adventuresome as his flock would wish, at least he is being strictly honourable. Even so, it is not his loyalty to Assyria that is responsible for the Prophet's make-your-bed-and-lie-in-it attitude, so much as his belief in the principle that God is to be trusted to bring order out of chaos. Again Isaias is showing himself to be the apostle of Abandonment. Fatalism, you say ? Oh, no ! *Kismet* is lying down and hoping for the best, *Fides* is working for the best and accepting what comes of it lying down. ' Wait for the Lord,' says Isaias. God does not forget His children. His children must wait for Him, but they must not go to sleep while doing so . . . ' *watch* and pray, lest ye enter into temptation,' not merely kill time in the delay— much less force a humanly devised solution to the difficulty. You Jews, you must learn to *trust* . . . to wait . . . to pray.

Isaias is not the first to urge upon the Jews submission to the *status quo ;* the Prophet's words would have come as naturally from the lips of Samuel. We can imagine the last of the judges telling those who came to him asking for a king that they have an

' Emmanuel '—what more should they require ?
Indeed there are several points in common between
Isaias and the Prophet Samuel : the same patriarchal
gravity, the same ' other-worldliness ' which shows
itself in a sublime indifference to royal sensibilities,
the same failure—humanly speaking—to win over the
masses to the way of God, and even (if the surmise
of modern scholars regarding Isaias's school of prophets
be correct) the same tendency to influence the young
and to found a religious body which will counter the
godlessness of the next generation.[1] Just as Samuel
rebuked Saul for taking it upon himself to ensure for
the safety of his people apart from God so Isaias does
the same. ' And when they shall say to you : Seek
of pythons and of diviners who mutter in their enchant-
ments ; should not the people seek of their God for
the living of the dead ? ' It is the age-old fickleness of
the Hebrew race that is at the bottom of all their evils ;
that which shows itself in superstition in one century
will show itself in ambition or the cultivation of
' unbelieving manners ' in another : the Jews will
never remember that they are a peculiar people,
subject to peculiar laws and safeguarded by a peculiar
Providence. They must look, the Prophet repeats for
the hundredth time, ' to the law, rather, and to the
testimony ; and if they speak not according to this
word, they shall not have the morning light.' And
listen to what will happen in the absence of that
' morning light ' : ' they shall fall and be hungry ;
and when they shall be hungry they shall be angry,
and shall curse their king and their God '—which, as

---

[1] v. 16 of ch. viii is quoted to show that Isaias had a ' group ' :
' seal the law among my disciples,' while in the case of Samuel
there is, of course, less doubt (1 Kings xii, 2).

we know, is what they did do—' and they shall look to the earth, and behold trouble and darkness, weakness and distress, and a mist following them, and they cannot fly away from their distress.'

What a perfect description is the above of what comes upon the soul that turns to earthly consolation in a time of spiritual trial ! We are so ready to seek advice from the strongholds of ' sound common sense ' when we ought to be on our knees asking for the morning light. We think we are so wise when we train ourselves with the textbooks of the world. Is it not that this kind of education is so much easier ? Sophism, cant, the fashionable, the generally-accepted, they are all so many sops thrown out to a mind that craves for truth but will be able to get on with half-truth. In default of the best we grasp at the second best ; in default of the spiritual we want to know all that can be known about the natural . . . ' they shall look to the earth, and behold trouble and darkness,' is it not always so—trouble and darkness—when we fail to look long enough in the direction of the light ? ' And a mist following them, and they cannot fly away from their distress.' The mist will surely follow us, hiding from us the beauties of God's creation and separating us from those who would follow our lead . . . for just so long as we refuse to yield to grace. When Isaias warns the Jews that they ' cannot fly away from their distress ' he is far from implying that they are doomed to darkness however penitent be their hearts ; what the Prophet means, surely, is that those who continue ' looking to the earth ' will never find it in them to fly into the arms of God.

One might conclude this section of Isaias's prophecies by saying that the world is doing to-day what Achaz

and the people of Jerusalem were doing seven hundred
years before Christ. ' Give us immediate results and
no responsibilities towards the future,' is what the
twentieth century is saying ; ' give us pleasure but not
babies ; give us interests but nothing so tedious as a life's
work ; give us appetizers but not appetites ; give us, in
short, just as much of this life as will enable us to forget
about the next . . . give us the earth, and the heavens
can look after themselves.' Do you wonder that there
is ' darkness ', ' weakness ', ' distress ', ' and a mist
following them ' ? Dark enough, certainly, is the
future . . . when all about us is weakness of purpose,
distress of mind, and mist of uncertainty. We have
only to look at twentieth-century marriage, twentieth-
century employment, twentieth-century property, education, family life, to see that we have inherited our
share of ' weakness ' and ' distress '—let alone the fog
of religious unbelief. Would we had an Isaias in our
pulpits to convince the world that a mist will inevitably
follow the theist who can do without Christ, the
Christian who can do without the Church, and the
Good-behaviourist who can do without prayer. ' And
they cannot fly away,' poor things, ' from their
distress '.

iv

If we abide by the plan of S. Jerome which refers
ch. vii–xiv, 28 to the reign of Achaz it would perhaps
be as well to conclude this section with a summary of
the chapters not yet accounted for ; thus in ch. ix the
Prophet is telling of a vision he has been granted of
the Messias ; in ch. x he reveals the plan of God in select-
ing Assyria for the punishment of Israel ; ch. xi is a

prophecy of the Kingdom ; to which discourse belongs ch. xii, a hymn of praise and thanksgiving ; chs. xiii and xiv are probably the notes of a later sermon, delivered first of all against Babylon and then against Assyria and the Philistines. These six chapters comprise the prophecies which belong to the four years 730–726. Chs. ix, xi, and xii are among the richest of Isaias's Messianic chapters, while ch. xiv is considered by some to be the finest piece of poetry in the whole of the Old Testament. If the reader will oblige me by going through the text of this section for himself—and I am confident that he will find himself amply rewarded for his virtue —I, for my part, will endeavour to lighten the burden by supplying the background to the prophecies in question.

The most outstanding personality of this period is, of course, Theglathphalasar. This monarch predeceased his Judean vassal, Achaz, by one year, dying in 727 after a career of unparalleled triumph. Having taken the throne by force (745) he welded the tired and dissipated Assyrian nation into a power of the first rank such as it had been before. Successful against Babylon in the first years of his rule he was equally successful on the Syrian side of his dominions, driving out one by one the kings or chieftains of the semi-detached Syrian provinces. Already by 738 Theglathphalasar was receiving tribute from southern Asia Minor and from a certain ' queen of Arabia ' ; from 737–735 he was concentrating his attention on Media and Armenia. In 734, having, as we have said, annexed the outlying Syrian provinces, Theglathphalasar laid siege to the heart of Syria itself—the city of Damascus. It took the Assyrian two years of expensive fighting to bring the capital to its knees ; Damascus fell (as Isaias had said it would) in 732.

This triumph was celebrated by the execution of the adventurer Rasin. Theglathphalasar then made Damascus his temporary headquarters, receiving there the tributes of Ammon, Moab, Ascalon, Gaza and Edom, all of which he had colonized in his fourteen years of rule. It was at Damascus and at about this time that Achaz came to meet his overlord, bringing with him the price—which was an exorbitant one—of peace. The occasion, as we know from 4 Kings xvi, was marked by the attraction which the Judean felt towards the Assyrian altar that had recently been erected in the city. Achaz expressed himself so enchanted with the design that he had architect's plans drawn up during his stay at Damascus, and an exact copy of the altar was finally placed in position in Jerusalem. I am tempted to enlarge upon this incident but, having written about it elsewhere and not being able at the moment to obtain a copy of the book in question, I am afraid of either repeating or contradicting myself. I am, however, perfectly safe in drawing a moral from the behaviour of the king of Juda on this occasion. The account in the Book of Kings is as follows :

'And king Achaz went to Damascus to meet Theglathphalasar king of the Assyrians, and when he had seen the altar of Damascus, king Achaz sent to Urias the priest a pattern of it, and its likeness according to all the work thereof. And Urias the priest built an altar according to all that king Achaz had commanded from Damascus, so did Urias the priest until king Achaz came from Damascus. And when the king was come from Damascus he saw the altar and worshipped it, and went up and offered holocausts and his own sacrifice.'

Now we know from the opening verses of this same chapter in Kings that Achaz was far from being the devout Temple-goer who appears in the above passage ; he was one who ' did according to the idols of the nations,' who even made his own son ' pass through the fire.' Whence, then, this sudden interest in Temple furniture ? Achaz has a way of cloaking his movements (or his refusals to move) under cover of religion. ' I will not tempt the Lord,' we have heard him say when the Prophet bids him ask for a sign, and now, when he wants to flatter Theglathphalasar, he pretends that he is all eagerness to do a service to religion. Achaz has no love of God, but he has something which is often mistaken for the love of God—a certain *flair* for ceremonial worship. Whether the worship be directed towards the Lord, towards nature, or towards idols, does not seem to matter much ; as long as Achaz can entertain himself with an emotional experience of a ' spiritual ' nature he feels he can pass himself off as a religious man. His son, Ezechias, will inherit something of this from his father, though, as we shall see in the next chapter, the failings of this far worthier king will amount to no more than a certain mild humbug and self-deception.

But perhaps I am doing even the father, Achaz, an injustice ; perhaps the king has persuaded himself that he is really serving God. But even if he has so persuaded himself, he is serving God in his own—and in a most unorthodox—way. *Quod volumus sanctum est* was supposed, according to S. Augustine, to be a claim of the Donatists ! There is the regrettable tendency in most of us to see things, not as they are in themselves, but as we are in *our*selves, fashioning and interpreting circumstance ' after our own image and

likeness '. Just as common as judging others by ourselves is the facility of judging ourselves as we like to
think that others judge us. It is conceivably possible,
therefore, that Achaz never intended to play the
hypocrite but that he had beatified himself from the
beginning. There is no limit to the extent of self-
justification ; a man can forge a chain in his mind
(and for every link he will show you the written test)
which is able to connect the most hopelessly
contradictory principles. Reader, do not deceive
yourself ; when you are in doubt look at those three
old inseparables : the subject, the object, and the end
. . . but look closest of all at the subject, because that
is *you*. And it is the *you* in every action that is likely
to colour everything else.

Now to return to Theglathphalasar.

With the fall of Samaria (not the final collapse of
that nation which took place in 722 at the hands of
Theglathphalasar's grandson, Sargon, but the annexa-
tion which it suffered together with its fellow-rebel,
Syria) a successor to Phacee was found by Theglathphalasar in the person of the Israelite prince, Osee.
This was the last ruler of the Northern Kingdom and
' he did evil before the Lord, but not as the kings of
Israel had done before him.' Theglathphalasar had
reason to regret the appointment of his nominee, because
Osee was misguided enough to rebel against him. The
Assyrian conqueror would undoubtedly have defeated
the Samaritan if he had lived long enough, but, as it was,
the final overthrow of Osee was delayed for five years.

It will be seen how history repeats itself : Osee,
who was as conscious of his inability to carry out a
successful rebellion against Assyria as Phacee had been
before him, enlisted the services of So, king of Egypt,

to assist him in his enterprise. He seems to have gained the half-hearted allegiance of Luli, king of Tyre, as well.[1] We shall see when we come to the next reign (which, dear reader, I promise you we shall do in time) with what difficulty it was that the suppression of Samaria and Tyre was ultimately effected. Not without a struggle did Israel yield for ever her place in history. It was easy enough to imprison Osee—even the weak Salmanasar V, Theglathphalasar's son, managed to do that—but it was reserved for Sargon, the next super-man in the Assyrian line of kings, to wipe out the nationality of the Northern People. Before leaving the thumbnail biography of Theglathphalasar it is worth while noticing that, having penetrated as far as Philistia when he came to Achaz's assistance, he had, by the time that he came to die, the whole of the Trans-Jordan and Galilee area under his control ; which, together with the Chaldean territory of which he became master in the last year of his life (assuming the name of Pul, king of Babylon), spreads the extent of Assyrian power from the Tigris to the Mediterranean shore.

A word now about those two *enfants terribles*, Rasin, king of Damascus (Syria), and Phacee, son of Romelia, king of Israel (Samaria).

[1] This Osee must have been something of a problem to his friends and enemies alike. He was put on to the throne in the first place because of his pro-Assyrian and anti-Phacee sympathies (Theglathphalasar being anxious to appoint native rulers wherever possible in his dominions), but, as we have seen, the appointment was a failure : Osee rebelled against the people of which he was a more or less—and rather more than less—favoured vassal. Osee must have had about ten years of nominal kingship, the last three of which were spent in prison. He was a sore disappointment to at least three nations, not to mention his own, and ' he did evil in the sight of the Lord.' The Book of Kings (which gives Osee nine years of rule and not ten) is unfortunately silent about his end.

We have seen how these princes first solicited
Achaz's help and then attacked him ; we have heard
what Isaias had to say about them—that they
were no more than firebrands, guttering torches ;
and lastly we have watched the Assyrian army
tread out their flame. It but remains, if we are
anxious to see how the Prophet's words were verified,
to account for the way in which each of them met his
death.

It is a pity that in spite of the frequent mention of
both names in the Book of Kings, in Isaias, and in
Assyrian monuments, no clear idea can be formed of
their personalities. Rasin was slain, as has been said,
when Damascus was laid waste, and Phacee followed
his friend two years later (730) when Theglathphalasar
mastered Samaria. Of the two, Rasin seems to have
been the more able general while Phacee excelled his
ally in unscrupulous conspiracy. The divine right of
kings meant nothing very much to either of them.
Phacee obtained his throne by the assassination of his
predecessor, Pheceia, and Rasin was made king as the
result of a general insurrection (which he had organized)
in the states of Syria. Both men were of the petty
chieftain stock (common even in the Palestine of
to-day) that delighted in war for its own sake, that
was as ready to juggle with crowns as with swords,
that was glad enough to make a splash in this life and
asked nothing in place of the next. ' A *mere* Rasin,'
says Isaias (whose outlook on life is far from frivolous),
' is head of Damascus . . . and the head of Samaria is
only Romelia's son.'[1] But they made their splash,

---

[1] Our version does not express the contempt suggested in the
above. I do not know how far the Revised Version is justified in
including the ' mere ' and the ' only.'

nevertheless, and things were considerably quieter in Palestine when they were gone.

It will be noticed that very little has been said about Babylonia, in spite of the fact that Isaias devotes an entire chapter (xiii) to the destruction of that nation. And though this prophecy falls within the section we have been considering and was undoubtedly delivered before the death of Achaz, I have presumed to omit the usual historical sketch in this case because of Babylon's quiescent part in the politics of the time. She had had a splendid past and was destined to come into her own again later on, but just at the time we are considering she was virtually an Assyrian colony. We reserve Babylon for fuller investigation when the reigns of Ezechias (of Juda), Sargon (of Assyria), and Shabaka (of Egypt) come under discussion.

Egypt has also received scant attention in the above review of Achaz's reign, but here I plead my subject, Isaias : except to hint that the day of Egypt is by no means done, and to prophesy the punishment of that people, Isaias is singularly reticent about Egypt in the first fourteen chapters of his Book. He is so much preoccupied with Assyria, and with telling the people of Jerusalem how wrong they are to be preoccupied with Rasin and Phacee, that he seems to have no time for the unbelieving nation of the south.

' Now the rest of the acts of Achaz which he did, are they not written in the Book of the words of the days of the kings of Juda ? And Achaz slept with his fathers and was buried with them in the city of David, and Ezechias his son reigned in his stead.'[1]

[1] 4 Kings xvi, 19, 20.

CHAPTER V

IN EZECHIAS'S REIGN

i

' In the third year of Osee the son of Ela king of Israel '—the appointment had been made, it will be remembered, by the king of Assyria—' reigned Ezechias the son of Achaz king of Juda. He was five and twenty years old when he began to reign, and he reigned nine and twenty years in Jerusalem ; the name of his mother was Abi the daughter of Zacharias.' This is from the Book of Kings.[1]

We are now in the year 726 B.C. Assyria is still adding strength to strength ; Juda and Syria—indeed all the states of Palestine—are more than uneasy in the yoke that is being forced upon them ; in the south Egypt is becoming restive, apprehending, as it must, the possibility of an Assyrian-cum-Syrian-cum-Chaldean-cum-Judean descent upon its borders ; Babylon, freed from the dominion of Theglathphalasar who has just died (727), but which still pays tribute to Assyria, is being secretly and very swiftly built up by the nationalist king Merodach-Baladan ; and king Osee in Israel is making a spirited bid for independence against Theglathphalasar's successor, Salmanasar V, king of Assyria.

---

[1] 4 Kings xviii, 1, 2. This and the two chapters following will be freely quoted from now onwards. The narrative portions of what follows is taken from Kings and not from the Prophecy of Isaias.

With such a situation before him the young king of Juda looks about—as his father had done sixteen years ago—for some sort of security as regards the future. Humanly speaking the outlook is as black as it has ever been, but fortunately Ezechias is a man of prayer and so is well prepared to accept the words of the court prophet, Isaias, which told him what has been told to his father before him—to trust in God; and since this sort of doctrine meets every kind of situation, the prospect, bad as it is, need cause the king no serious alarm. Still, he must take the ordinary precautions— if there be any. Let him see, now, Philistia . . . what of Philistia ? No hope in that direction, Philistia is smarting under the blows received from the late Theglathphalasar. Nor can Ezechias trust in his erstwhile enemy Samaria, for Osee, its sovereign, is being chased about the country by Salmanasar. Syria, with its fair Damascus in ruins, may not be counted on for many a year to come. Babylon . . . what of Babylon ? But no, she is, for all practical purposes, as Assyrian as Nineveh itself (Ezechias has not yet learned of Merodach-Baladan's activities). There is only one race left : Egypt . . . how would Egypt serve if Assyria were suddenly to turn hostile ? Ezechias must consider Egypt seriously, because the time may come when Salmanasar will want more than Juda's present tribute . . . and Ezechias doubts very much if his people can be further taxed . . . yes, Egypt is certainly worth a thought.

And so we can imagine the young king, after making discreet enquiries and calculating what will be the state of Juda's finances in ten years' time, sending for Isaias with a view to hearing any further suggestions which might possibly be brought to bear.

F

With Isaias seated at a table in front of him, some such speech as this might not unreasonably be attributed to the king :

' My friend, we have need of all the prayers we can get. Just look at this map a minute. And when you have studied the geographical aspect of the situation to your satisfaction I would ask you to glance at this balance sheet which I have had drawn up. Now I must tell you that I would no more trust this Salmanasar than I would have trusted our late friends, Rasin and Phacee ; with the father, Theglathphalasar, it was different—he was really great—but with the new man . . . well, what is to keep him to his predecessor's agreement ? He may demand what little my father left behind. There is, however, this to be thankful for : the Assyrians are afraid of Egypt. How would it be if we were to make friends with the Egyptians ? Nothing in the way of a settled pact, of course, because after all they are a heathen people . . . but with their assurance of goodwill we should be in a position to refuse any demands for money which Assyria might feel inclined to make. And then if we could mention the fact that Syria and, say, Babylonia were equally disposed to lean on the friendship of Egypt, why, Salmanasar would think twice about asking us to " meet " his travelling expenses ! Think it over, O Prophet, and let me have your opinion in a day or two.'

But Isaias needs no time to think it over. What does he think of Egypt, does the king want to know ? This is what Isaias thinks of Egypt—and then comes ch. xix ! Egypt a possible ally ? Egypt is a quite *im*possible ally, ' Egypt is man and not God.'[1]

---

[1] Cf. xxxi, 3.

So the suggestion is turned down and nothing more is heard of the proposed friendship for some fourteen years or more. Sennacherib will then be upon the Assyrian throne, and, moreover, the situation, regarding Syria and Babylonia will be considerably altered . . . but the thoughts that have occurred to the king's mind in the early days of his reign and which have been peremptorily dealt with by Isaias are just the thoughts that would appeal to the timorous, fickle, untrusting people of Jerusalem, and we shall see on a later page how powerful the ' Egyptian party ' has become in Juda when we come to the next political crisis.

And of Egypt herself meanwhile ? The first we hear of Egypt's part in the politics of the time is the reference (in 4 Kings xvii, 4) to king Osee's embassy asking the help of Sua in his attempt to throw off the yoke of Assyria. This Sua, or Sabako, or Shebek, was an Ethiopian prince who had risen to power quite recently and who was busy at this time in doing for Egypt what Merodach-Baladan was doing for Babylon : Sua was founding a new dynasty, the twenty-fifth. It is true that the age of triumphant Pharaohs was past, the age when even Assyria and Chaldea kept anxious eyes on the eastern banks of the Nile, but Egypt had never yet been defeated and a legend had somehow gathered round her that she was incapable of suffering defeat. Isaias did not believe in this legend. Another thing about Egypt which proved misleading to those who were trying to assess her strength was the fact that her courts were as magnificent as ever before and her armies as splendidly equipped . . . but was there any *power* behind it all ? Wealth there was, certainly, as the caravans on the trade-route testified, and the learning of Egypt's wise men seems also to have been

universally recognized at this time . . . but military
prowess ? No one knew. Last of all to suspect the
passing of Egypt's greatness were the Egyptians
themselves. With the result that when the question
came up of joining forces with the principalities of
Palestine and Syria against their traditional rivals,
the Assyrians, the leading statesmen in Egypt pressed
for war. The Nile valley had high hopes of the young
Ethiopian, Sua, and Theglathphalasar's successor was
seen to be but a feeble reflection of his father . . . so
why not ? Unfortunately for Egypt it was Sargon,
and not Salmanasar, with whom they had to reckon
when they ultimately embarked upon war. And Sargon
proved more than a match for the enterprising and able
Sua. But we are anticipating. We shall meet Sua
again in two years' time (720) at the battle of Raphia,
when we can indulge in a glance at his private history ;
our immediate business is to ascertain the attitudes of
the remaining nations in regard to those whose attitudes
we know already, namely, Juda, Assyria, and Egypt.
How, for example, does the bruised and battered—but
not altogether broken—Philistia view the situation ?
How does Syria—as changeable a nation as Juda
itself—regard Egypt ? And Babylon, with Merodach-
Baladan at the helm, where is she in all this ?

We can only account for the astonishing self-
confidence which led these three nations to take their
places again in the theatre of war by putting it down
to the effect of Theglathphalasar's death upon the then
known world. The pressure of this one man's personality once relieved, all were jumping at each other's
throats again. But it was only for a glorious five
years ! Sargon was another, and an even greater,
Theglathphalasar.

First of all, Philistia : we do not know what proportion of the Philistines was still sufficiently warworthy after the campaigns of the previous decade, but certainly Gaza, and possibly also some of the lesser tribes, joined forces with Sua and the Egyptians in an attempt to overthrow Assyria. This was just about the time that Salmanasar died. Sargon, marching south over the ashes of Samaria (and presumably also over the grave of Osee whom he slew on becoming king), met the combined forces at Raphia in 720, effecting a victory which was to keep Egypt quiet for fifteen years. Sua was taken and killed. Egypt, therefore, was ruled out for the time being from the hopes of Juda. What was left of the Egyptian forces retreated the way they had come, and Sargon contented himself with halting at Raphia. This was the second of Sargon's signal triumphs and he had only been on the throne two years. Juda trembled; Syria—what remained of it—also trembled; Babylon did not tremble.

Before we leave Egypt to his successor, Tirhaka (or whoever it was that came between Sua and Tirhaka in the line of kings[1]), a word is perhaps not out of place on the Ethiopian who very nearly restored to Egypt her ancient glory.

Sua, about whose identity there is still confusion (some refusing to allow that he is the originator of the Ethiopian dynasty, and claiming therefore that ' Sibe ' and ' Shabaka ' are two different people), obtained the throne of Egypt by burning his predecessor alive. The doubtful claim which he made to royal blood seems to have been accepted by the masses in the delta provinces, while he managed to persuade his own people, the Southerners, that their interests were his one concern.

[1] Authorities are not unanimous about the succession.

Having created chaos in the kingdom, he proceeded with great skill to introduce order . . . and by that time it was too late to turn him out ! Besides which, Egypt seems to have been only too pleased to find a leader—credentials or no credentials. From home affairs Sua turned himself to foreign policy with, as we have seen, less happy results. One would like to know how Sua, who must have been an attractive scoundrel in many ways, met his death ; I feel sure he had plenty to say to Sargon . . . and from what we know of Sargon, I should think the Egyptian was probably listened to with a lively interest.

With regard to Syria—that other thorn in Assyria's flesh—the Old Testament is singularly reticent ; nor do Assyrian monuments appear to provide any information which can help us to read the thoughts of Damascus at this time. We must therefore suppose that the Assyrian court which Theglathphalasar had established in the capital (732) was still flourishing, and that the Syria of former times gradually lost its nationality, becoming merged in the greater power. Whatever hopes were entertained in Jerusalem of threatening Assyria with a Judean-Syrian combine must have evaporated as Ezechias's reign progressed, because by the time that Babylon was suing for Juda's hand there was none who advocated the pro-Syrian policy that had so nearly gained the day in Achaz's reign. Thus Syria need not be mentioned again.

Far different is the case of Babylon. Let me preface my remarks about the relations between this nation and Juda by saying at once that there is a chronological difficulty which obscures the view of Babylon in the most maddening way. We have it on the authority of the Fourth Book of Kings that Sennacherib (Sargon's

successor of whom more later, we have not come to
the end of Sargon as yet) came up against Juda in the
' fourteenth year of king Ezechias ' and was defeated
by the People of the Lord. This was the vindication
of a very direct prophecy on the part of Isaias (xxxvi–
xxxviii), and is an historical fact, recorded in 2 Parali-
pomenon xxxii, 1, as well as in the historical records
of Assyria. Now in the ' fourteenth year of Ezechias's
reign '—in other words 712 B.C.—Sennacherib was not
on the throne of Assyria ; Sargon did not die until 705.
Now though the *fact* of Assyria's defeat is chronicled
as stated above, the *date* is given in Kings alone.
When we look for something that *did* take place in
the ' fourteenth year of Ezechias's reign ' we find, of
course, that this was when he first got ill, and when
it was promised him, through Isaias, that he would
live another fifteen years—which he did, dying in
697. And so the authorities (with that genius they
show for picking upon the absent-mindedness of
scribes) would have it that the words ' in the fourteenth
year of Ezechias's reign ' were tacked on to the wrong
incident. If this be so, all I ask is : how then did
Isaias, who after all was present in Jerusalem for both
incidents (and very much present in the sick-room
incident), get them wrong ? Mind you, I do not
pretend to know the answer, I merely say that Isaias
tells first of Sennacherib's defeat and then of the
coming of Babylon's ambassadors (which we know took
place at the end of Ezechias's illness). I have read
the explanations but I cannot say that I am impressed ;
not sufficiently impressed, at all events, to reproduce
them here. I leave it at that : there is a chronological
difficulty at this juncture which is (to my mind)
simply maddening. So what I propose to do here is

to shelve the Sennacherib invasion until that monarch
is definitely upon the throne of Assyria,[1] and treat
here of Ezechias's sickness and its sequel—the arrival
of Merodach-Baladan's legates.

ii

'In those days Ezechias was sick unto death ; and
Isaias the son of Amos the prophet came to him and
said : Thus saith the Lord God : Give charge concerning thy house for thou shalt die and not live. And
he turned his face to the wall and prayed to the Lord,
saying : I beseech Thee, O Lord, remember how I
walked before Thee in truth and with a perfect heart,
and have done that which is pleasing before Thee.
And Ezechias wept with much weeping. And before
Isaias was gone out of the middle of the court, the
word of the Lord came to him saying : Go back and
tell Ezechias the captain of My people : Thus saith
the Lord, the God of David thy father : I have heard
thy prayer and I have seen thy tears, and behold I
have healed thee ; on the third day thou shalt go up
to the Temple of the Lord. And I will add to thy days
fifteen years.'

And really, when we read the chapter but one
before this, we have to admit that the king deserved
to have his prayers heard if anyone did. The Book of
Kings (Fourth Book, ch. xviii) reveals a thoroughly
noble type in the person of Ezechias, all the more
worthy on account of the miserable specimens who
have occupied the throne before him. Think how
Isaias must have delighted in the improved state of
things under the reforming king. The early years

[1] See Appendix I.

of Ezechias's reign were enough to inspire the rosiest of hopes, and even had Jeremias been in Isaias's place one ventures to think that the prophecies of this period must have been pitched in a cheerful key.

' He [Ezechias] destroyed the high places and broke the statues in pieces, and cut down the groves and broke the brazen serpent . . . he trusted in the Lord the God of Israel so that after him there was none like him among all the kings of Juda, nor any of them that were before him '—which is a slight overstatement because Josias, his great-grandson, was considered every bit as godly a king—' and he stuck to the Lord, and departed not from His steps, but kept His commandments which the Lord commanded Moses. Wherefore the Lord also was with him.' So we are not surprised that the Lord should hear his prayer for a longer life. What does surprise us, perhaps, is the Isaias who is pictured in the Book of Kings. Listen to what happens when the Prophet gets back to the royal bedside :

' And Isaias said : Bring me a lump of figs. And when they had brought it and laid it upon his boil he was healed. And Ezechias said to Isaias : What shall be a sign that the Lord will heal me and that I shall go up to the Temple of the Lord the third day ? And Isaias said to him : This shall be a sign to thee from the Lord that the Lord will do the word which He hath spoken : Wilt thou that the shadow go forward ten lines or that it go back so many degrees ? And Ezechias said : It is an easy matter that the shadow go forward ten lines '—once promised a miracle the king sees no reason why he should not have a first-class miracle . . . he will have all the more to thank God for when he goes up to the Temple in three days' time—' and I do not desire that this be done, but let

it return back ten degrees. And Isaias the Prophet
called upon the Lord and He brought the shadow
ten degrees backwards by the lines by which it had
already gone down in the dial of Achaz.' I do not
know if the reader will agree with me but this terse
Isaias—this ' fetch-me-figs,' this ' I'll-show-you-that-
the-Lord-is-as-good-as-His-word ' Isaias—is somehow
not the kind of man one would expect from his writings.
Perhaps the author of this part of the Book of Kings
did not know his Isaias to speak to, or had not read
the prophecies that had already been published . . .
possibly a stern, downright, taciturn, Elias-like prophet
was considered more fitting ; also, the important
figure of the sick-room story being Ezechias rather
than Isaias, it was thought (perhaps) that not too much
attention must be paid to the Prophet. At all events
that is the only way I can justify the subduing of
Isaias's ready eloquence. One would have thought
that the occasion would have called for something
rather special in the way of a homily ; after all, the
Prophet had given free enough rein in his dealing with
Achaz at the ' upper pool ' . . . and here, in Ezechias,
was a man he admired. Let us hope that he was curt
with his friend because he knew he could trust him ;
and because he thought, also, that his friend was
behaving somewhat childishly. . . .

iii

In the Book of Kings the sequel to this story of the
petulant invalid comes immediately afterwards :

' At that time Berodach Baladan,[1] the son of

---

[1] We have referred to him hitherto as Merodach-Baladan as
being the more usually accepted rendering of the name.

Baladan, king of the Babylonians, sent letters and presents to Ezechias, for he had heard that Ezechias had been sick. And Ezechias rejoiced at their coming, and he showed them the house of his aromatical spices, and the gold and the silver, and divers precious odours and ointments, and the house of his vessels, and all that he had in his treasures. There was nothing in his house nor in all his dominions that Ezechias showed them not.'

This is an exceedingly interesting passage because besides showing us what a silly person Ezechias was in many ways—open to flattery and inclined to show off—it provides us with two important pieces of information : first, that there was still a certain amount in the treasury that was worth showing ; and second, that the Babylonian ambassadors took very good care to see all that there was to be seen. Ostensibly arriving at the court of Juda to inquire after the king's health, Baladan's ministers had obviously been instructed beforehand to assess the value of Juda from the point of view of a possible alliance in the future. The Babylonian nationalist king, we must remember, was busy buoying up the spirits of Chaldea, and it would be useful to him if he could say, on his ministers' return from their corporal work of mercy, that his friends the Judeans were nothing like as poor as they were stated to be on the Assyrian tribute rolls. And again, should Judea by any unfortunate chance decide to further the Assyrian cause, well, it was useful to know what resources they had at the back of them.

You see, dear reader, one thing was quite certain : Babylon was determined to fight it out with Assyria. And you will see also why it was that Isaias, in the

verses that immediately follow, was so angry with the
king for his more than crass stupidity and vanity.
Isaias saw through the tender inquiries of the Babylonian legates.

' And Isaias the Prophet came to king Ezechias and
said to him : What said these men ? or from whence
came they to thee ? And Ezechias said to him : From
a far country they came to me out of Babylon ' (wasn't
it nice of them—all that way ?), ' and he [Isaias] said :
What did they see in thy house ? And Ezechias said :
They saw all the things that are in my house ; there
is nothing among my treasures that I have not shown
them.' O the folly of display ! ' And Isaias said to
Ezechias : Hear the word of the Lord : Behold the
days shall come that all that is in thy house, and thy
fathers have laid up in store until this day, shall be
carried into Babylon : nothing shall be left, saith the
Lord.' And Isaias further predicts a like fate to
the seed of Ezechias. (We notice, incidentally, that the
writer of 4 Kings is letting the Prophet speak out a
little more !)

' Ezechias said to Isaias : The word of the Lord
which thou hast spoken is good ; let peace and truth
be in my days.' So the king repents him of his in-
discretion and bows beneath the heavy hand of God.
Ezechias is an admirable person when it comes to the
important things of life ; it is only that he is easily
carried away in the unessentials.

' And the rest of the acts of Ezechias,' the text
continues, ' and all his might . . . are they not written
in the book of the words of the days, etc.,' which would
lead us to believe, on the face of it, that this was the
end of Ezechias. Whereas, of course, he had those
fifteen more years of life, and—but we must go back

two chapters to get at them—those badly chronicled encounters with Sennacherib.

iv

Just, first of all, to get our bearings with regard to dates. If Ezechias's illness is given to the year 712 then one more year of peace can be attributed to Juda before Sargon, who has been occupying himself with a war on his northern frontier against Armenia for the last two years, brings pressure to bear upon his none too docile vassal. As to what form this hostile interest in Juda's affairs took we have no opportunity of knowing : Assyrian records claim for the year 711 the successful quashing of revolts from Philistia, Edom, Moab, and Juda. We know from other sources that Sargon stormed Azotus (Philistia) in this year and took captive a vast number of Philistines, but beyond the words ' He [Ezechias] rebelled against the king of the Assyrians and served him not,' there is nothing to show for this supposed passage of arms between the two nations. Purposely do I use the word ' nations ' here because Juda's status as an independent people —though technically subject to Assyria—is gradually being reasserted. Juda's position in the eyes of the surrounding powers is clearly seen from the passage next to be quoted. It is, of course, not difficult to estimate the value of Juda's support, once Juda is able to support—and defend—herself. Assyria, for example, would be placing herself in a difficult position strategically if, in an attack upon Egypt, she had not the friendship of a now well-equipped Juda to count upon ; Juda might easily bear down upon the Assyrian armies in the rear and cut off all hope of a retreat.

The same would apply to an Egyptian army marching
north against Assyria. And as for Babylon, Merodach-
Baladan, having assured himself of Judean securities,
was prepared to risk a good deal in bidding for the
favour of the Chosen People : he risked the disfavour
of the Assyrian king at a time when it was absolutely
necessary to his cause that Assyria should not concern
herself with the private affairs of Babylon ; it was
only by his being a ' dark horse ' that Merodach-
Baladan had managed to remain in the stable.

By 705, which is the date of Sargon's death and the
beginning of Sennacherib's reign, Jerusalem had
become a political market. Tirhaka (or ' Theraca ' as
he is called in the Book of Kings), Sua's brother-in-law
and still king of Egypt, was contemplating a renewal
of hostilities with Assyria and was evidently under
the impression that the battle of Raphia had not been
so decisive after all. At any rate he believed in the
principle of attack being the best defence, with the
result that he urged with Ezechias the necessity of
breaking with the Assyrian domination while the
new Assyrian king was still finding his feet. It was
an unfortunate thing for the Egyptians that whenever
they were congratulating themselves on the death of
a great Assyrian a still greater Assyrian was in the act
of taking over the reins. Sennacherib was certainly in
the tradition of Theglathphalasar and Sargon. He
very soon discovered, for example, the game that
Merodach-Baladan had been playing ; he knew also
of Tirhaka's flirtation with Juda. With the result
that he

' Sent Tharthan and Rabsaris and Rabsaces from
Lachis to king Ezechias with a strong army to Jerusalem ; and they went up and came to Jerusalem, and

they stood by the conduit of the upper pool which is
in the way of the fuller's field. And they called for the
king.' Ezechias, very wisely, did not go. He did
what—being the kind of man he was—was a much more
sensible thing to do than attending open-air parleys :
he went into the Temple and prayed. Apart from the
direct value of his prayer, and apart also from the
value which his people derived from his act in the way
of edification, there was (in my very humble opinion)
another reason for his non-appearance which I shall
venture to put forward in a minute. ' And there went
out to them Eliacim the son of Helcias who was over
the house, and Sobna the scribe, and Joahe the son
of Asaph the recorder.'

We must interrupt the quotation (which I guarantee
the reader will enjoy enormously—and all the more so
for this present interruption) in order to see who these
people were that took the king's place at the discussion,
and why it was that they were chosen to do so.

Just as in Achaz's reign there had been three political
parties in Jerusalem—the pro-Assyrian, the pro-
Syrian, and the ' nationalist '—so now too there were
three parties in the kingdom, and the three names
chosen to represent Juda at the conduit assembly were
the leaders of those three parties. Here, surely, is the
other reason why Ezechias chose to stay away : he
shrank from foisting any private view of his own upon
the nation. Ezechias is a democrat. If this suggestion
is anywhere near the truth it will be readily seen in
what a delicate mould the conscience of the king
was cast.

Perhaps we are surprised to find that Isaias is not
among the delegates. The only reason (that I can
think of) for his not being chosen by Ezechias would

be this : the Prophet had by this time disassociated himself with party politics and had assumed the rôle of spiritual adviser of the king and—when necessary —of the nation. True, occasion might arise when, as now, there might be questions involving political knowledge to be decided, in which case Isaias would be called upon to give his advice ; but in the ordinary way (I take it) the Prophet would not appear in the political arena, confining himself instead to the pulpit and to his place in the council-chamber. That Isaias enjoyed a considerable following, however, in spite of his reticence is clear from the fact that Eliacim, who shared his views, appears as one of the spokesmen of the nation.

The three men represented the following trends of thought :

Eliacim, with the Prophet at his back, was for ' national independence.' He thought that Juda was now strong enough to defy both Assyria and Egypt ; further, he knew that he could depend upon the help of one or other of these nations—whichever chose not to attack. Isaias would have gone one better, repeating that ' in quietness and confidence shall your strength be.' ' Forget about possible alliances,' would have been the advice of the Prophet, ' trust simply in the Providence of God.' In pressing the cause of non-intervention Isaias was only being consistent with the line he had taken hitherto : when Samaria had threatened he had said ' Do not fight ' ; when Samaria and Syria had solicited . . . the same thing. Now, with Assyria forcing a crisis at the very doors of Jerusalem, his message was identical. And see how successful it had been before ! Juda remained the one solitary state that had escaped devastation. No

one could have foreseen, twenty years before, that the
rise of Babylon as a new force would turn the tide of
Juda's fortunes. No one could have said, twenty
years before—when Juda was in danger of becoming
the cockpit of Palestine—that the time would come
(and that so soon) when the three great powers would
be vying with each other for Juda's smiles !

Sobna the scribe favoured Egypt. He was fiercely
attacked by Isaias for so doing. Five verses are
devoted to Sobna in the Prophet's vitriolic twenty-
second chapter. Isaias foretells no good of Sobna the
scribe and, sure enough, he *is* ' driven out,' eventually,
' from his station, and deposed from his ministry.' It
is strange to think that, for all Isaias's warnings about
the evil of trusting to Egypt, it was this man Sobna's
party that ultimately carried the day : the encouragement given to Egypt was responsible for Assyria's
invasion of that land ; 701 was to show that Egypt
was indeed a ' broken reed.' At the time of the present
parley Ezechias was himself coquetting with the idea
of a pact with Tirhaka against Sennacherib.

Joahe, the son of Asaph the recorder, was pro-
Assyrian. That Joahe's followers were fairly numerous,
but that they were an obedient, law-abiding lot, is
seen from the quotation from the Book of Kings which
we began and then interrupted :

' And Rabsaces [Sennacherib's officer] said to them :
Speak to Ezechias : Thus saith the great king, the
king of the Assyrians : What is this confidence in
which thou trustest ? Perhaps thou hast taken counsel
to prepare thyself for battle. On whom dost thou
trust that thou darest to rebel ? Dost thou trust in
Egypt, a staff of a broken reed, on which if a man
lean it will break and go into his hand and pierce it ?

G

So is Pharaoh king of Egypt to all that trust in him '
—the speaker is thinking of the battle of Raphia at
which he had probably been present, and is predicting,
incidentally, the battle of Eltekeh, where ' Pharaoh '
will show once for all that he is not to be leant upon
—' but if you say to me : We trust in the Lord our
God, is it not He whose altars and high places Ezechias
hath taken away ? And hath commanded Juda and
Jerusalem : You shall worship before this altar in
Jerusalem ? ' This is a strange thrust at the absent
king. Rabsaces has obviously heard something of the
reforming activities of Ezechias (the quoting as a
popular slogan ' We trust in the Lord our God ' shows
that Isaias had at least been listened to—and broad-
cast !), but he gets the reports confused : to the
Assyrian mind such a thing as the cutting down of
' groves ' implies a curtailing of religious worship ;
Rabsaces has not grasped the monotheistic idea. He
knows that the Hebrew has a highly religious nature,
and so if Sennacherib is to be successful Ezechias must
be shown up as the enemy of traditional worship.

' Now therefore,' continues the legate, ' come over
to my master the king of the Assyrians, and I will
give you two thousand horses and see whether you be
able to have riders for them. And how can you stand
against one lord of the least of my master's servants ?
Dost thou trust in Egypt for chariots and horsemen ? '
Notice that he harks back to Egypt each time, knowing
presumably that Ezechias is partial to the ' Pharaoh ' ;
he does not seem to consider Merodach-Baladan as a
serious rival. And now another appeal—on spiritual
grounds :

' Is it without the will of the Lord that I am come
up to this place to destroy it ? The Lord said to me :

Go up to this land and destroy it.' The man is a liar,
of course, but it is an unfortunate thing that he has
hit upon just that lie which can be taken to lend
colour to the prophecies of Isaias. Had not the
Prophet told Jerusalem again and again that Assyria
was being raised up by God to be the instrument of
their correction ?

The Hebrew ministers see that Rabsaces has scored
an important point.

' Then Eliacim the son of Helcias, and Sobna, and
Joahe said to Rabsaces : We pray thee speak to us
thy servants in Syriac, for we understand that tongue ;
and speak not to us in the Jews' language in the
hearing of the people that are upon the wall.' It is
obviously in a panic that this rather shabby suggestion
is made. The Assyrian, who shows himself to be
astuteness itself throughout the conference, is not slow
to see the weakness exhibited in the opposition and,
quite legitimately, takes advantage of it :

' And Rabsaces answered them saying : Hath my
master sent me to thy master and to thee to speak
these words, and not rather to the men that sit upon
the wall ? . . . Then Rabsaces stood and cried out with
a loud voice in the Jews' language and said : Hear the
words of the great king, the king of the Assyrians.
Thus saith the king : Let not Ezechias deceive you,
for he shall not be able to deliver you out of my hand.
Neither let him make you trust in the Lord saying :
The Lord will surely deliver us, and this city shall not
be given into the hands of the king of the Assyrians.
Do not hearken to Ezechias. For thus saith the king
of the Assyrians : Do with me that which is for your
advantage, and come out to me. And every man of
you shall eat of his own vineyard and of his own fig-

tree, and you shall drink water of your own cisterns.'
This is another particularly happy reference—the
back-to-the-land suggestion ; a return to agriculture
is a movement dear to the heart of the revered Prophet
as we shall see later on ; the Jews have been encouraged
to toil for just such a state of things as is held out to
them by this accommodating neighbour, Sennacherib !
' Till I come,' goes on Rabsaces on behalf of Sennacherib (and here the minister, seeing that he is winning
sympathy every moment, allows himself to become
somewhat lyrical) . . . ' till I come and take you away
to a land like to your own land, a fruitful land and
plentiful in wine, a land of bread and vineyards, a land
of olives and oil and honey, and you shall live and not
die. Hearken not to Ezechias who deceiveth you
saying : The Lord will deliver us.' Rabsaces is careful
not to mention any unclean foods in his list of the
kinds of *ambrosia* that are produced at home. Useful as
it is to dangle pleasing pictures before the eyes of his
public it will be well to end up by sketching in the
shadows : ' The Lord will deliver you ?—*Will* He,
though ? ' And so he goes on :

' Have any of the gods of the nations delivered their
land from the hand of the king of Assyria ? Where
is the god of Emath and of Arphad ? Where is the
god of Sepharvaim, of Ana, and of Ava ? Have they
delivered Samaria out of my hand ? '

Rabsaces is a genius ! We are not at all surprised
to learn that immediately following the above rather
one-sided discussion, ' Eliacim the son of Helcias who
was over the house, and Sobna the scribe, and Joahe
the son of Asaph the recorder, came to Ezechias with
their garments rent, and told him the words of Rabsaces.' The thing had been a dismal failure . . . if

only the king had been there . . . what the people on
the wall must be thinking goodness only knows . . .
and yet one wonders whether even Isaias would have
cut a more dignified figure . . . will not the king ask
the Prophet what he thinks should be done ? —

' And he sent Eliacim who was over the house, and
Sobna the scribe, and the ancients of the priests, covered
with sackcloths, to Isaias the Prophet the son of Amos ;
and they said to him : Thus saith Ezechias : This day
is a day of tribulation, and of rebuke, and of blasphemy
. . . it may be that the Lord thy God will hear the words
of Rabsaces, whom the king of the Assyrians his master
hath sent to reproach the living God, and to reprove
with words, which the Lord thy God hath heard ; and
do thou offer prayer for the remnants that are found.
So the servants of the king came to Isaias. And
Isaias said to them : Thus shall you say to your
master : Thus saith the Lord : Be not afraid for the
words which thou hast heard, with which the servants
of the king of the Assyrians have blasphemed me.'

We are not told of the effect that this message had
upon the king. Ezechias was such a devout man that
it probably never entered his head to find fault with the
Prophet's doctrine of submission—at any rate he did
not express whatever doubts he may have had—but
unless he was more than human the temptation must
have come to him to throw over this hesitating Prophet
of his. ' It's not the slightest use,' we can imagine
Ezechias saying to himself, ' my asking Isaias's advice ;
he always says exactly the same thing, and this everlasting " Wait, wait, wait " is bound to land us in
difficulties sooner or later. He has said himself that
Assyria will ultimately spoil the country of Juda ; why
should I see it happen in my time ? Here are the

Egyptians only wanting to be asked . . . here are the
Chaldeans who, with Merodach-Baladan whipping
them up into a patriotic frenzy, would jump at the
chance of a general revolt . . . and then Isaias says I
must be quiet ! It is indeed hard, and I know now
what my poor father must have had to endure at this
Prophet's hands.'

And his troubles were by no means over yet. Shortly
after the Rabsaces mission a letter came to the court
of Juda from Sennacherib which crossed the t's and
dotted the i's of all that the Assyrian legate had said.
Ezechias, making an act of faith that must redound
to his eternal credit, took the enemy's ultimatum into
the Temple, ' spread it before the Lord,' and prayed
a prayer that might almost have been dictated by
Isaias himself. He cast the whole care of his people
upon God.

' And Isaias the son of Amos sent to Ezechias saying :
Thus saith the Lord the God of Israel : I have heard
the prayer thou hast made to me concerning Sennacherib king of the Assyrians.' The message of the
Lord went on to say that Sennacherib would never
enter the Holy City and that Ezechias need have no
fear.

' And it came to pass that night that an angel of the
Lord came and slew in the camp of the Assyrians a
hundred and eighty-five thousand . . . and Sennacherib
king of the Assyrians departing went away, and he
returned and abode in Nineveh. And as he was
worshipping in the temple of Nesroch his god, Adram-
elech and Sarasar his sons slew him with the sword,
and they fled into the land of the Armenians, and
Asarhaddon his son reigned in his stead.' But this,
the assassination of Sennacherib, was not until a long

time after the abortive siege of Jerusalem; Sennacherib was murdered in 681. The writer of the
Book of Kings has a fine disregard of time; there is
much that must be filled in before we come to the end
of Sennacherib.[1]

As a sequel to the incidents above recorded it is
worthy of mention that Sobna was withdrawn from
office shortly afterwards. By the year 701, the date
of Egypt's final defeat and of those prophecies contained
in Isaias xxxvi and xxxvii, Sobna's place in the king's
household was occupied by Eliacim. This means that
Ezechias had by that time identified himself officially
—whatever views he may have held in private—with
the 'independent nationalists,' the party that trusted
in the advice of Isaias. The battle of Eltekeh settled
the question of siding or not siding with Egypt; Sobna
passed out of public life. Whether that official in fact
suffered the fate predicted of him we do not know;
it is the only occasion on which Isaias pronounced
sentence on a single individual. Sobna was a Syrian,
not a Jew.

v

There is peace again for Juda. Ezechias devotes
himself to the encouragement of husbandry, of study,
and of the arts. A crisis has passed.

I wonder if at this point I may digress? And draw
the parallel between Juda and the human soul?
There seems to be such a very distinct likeness in the

[1] Now that I have come to the end of this particular sequence
of events I feel that it is the place to make my excuses for dealing
with passages which I have dealt with at some length elsewhere
(in *Prophets and Princes*). My grounds for revisiting old scenes are
simply that I have come upon the upper pool from a completely
different angle. But, even so, there is inevitably a certain amount
of repetition.

workings of grace—whether with individuals or with
nations—that perhaps I may be pardoned for calling
up once again the happenings which have occupied us
hitherto. And then if my reader is not interested in
his soul (or in mine, or in anyone else's) he can
leave out this section altogether and go straight on to
section vi.

We have seen how, not once but several times, the
Chosen People have been faced with exactly the same
problem. The identical temptation seems to attack
the identical weakness ; does it mean that because
they have never really grappled with their ' pre-
dominant sin ' and cast it from them that the occasion
of it recurs, and will recur, until they do ? Or does
it mean that, made the way they are, the tests to
which they are subjected are always likely to be met
with again—whether successfully ' grappled with ' or
no ? I admit that I have not the faintest idea as to
the answer of this question, but I am sure that if
answer there be, the solution must coincide with whatever results from a parallel investigation of the soul of
man. It will not be the historian, or even the race-
psychologist who will tell me what I want, it is far
more likely to be the ordinary, practical, common-
sense mystic.

Put it this way : are not most souls conscious—
souls, I mean, who are definitely trying to lead the
spiritual life but who are not necessarily by any means
' perfect '—that the course which they have embarked
upon, thinking it was going to be so smooth, is in fact
nothing but one crisis after another ? And that each
crisis is very much like the one that went before ?
Where a steady growth of love is aimed at there is
almost invariably check, increased effort, climax . . .

and then—for a time—repose. Apparently it is in
the nature of the love of God to demand repeated
choices on the part of those who would walk by its
way. These 'choices' differ only in degree ; that is
to say their place on the scale of renunciation is variable,
but always the *nature* of the renunciation is the same.
The faculty, or virtue, or act, which is drawn upon
by the operation of grace is just that faculty, or virtue,
or act, which at all cost must not be buried in the
napkin (I use the word ' act ' in its theological sense,
of course ; but even so I doubt if it admits of burial
in napkins). In fact one might go so far as to say that
the repeated eliciting of one particular quality of act
may be taken as a fair indication that it is just in the
direction of that act that sanctification must be
sought, and in no other. It will be in that direction
also that the soul's greatest dangers will lie.

I quote here an anonymous writer whose words
would seem to have a direct bearing upon the above :
'Thus [the soul perceived that] if the will was
required to accept a certain uncongenial work, then
the accepting of uncongenial works would form the
material of the succeeding struggle. Or again, [that]
if the understanding was being pressed to renounce a
certain judgement, then the renunciation of judgement
would be demanded of the understanding on another,
and a more vital, issue.' The same writer goes on to
describe the case of a soul who ' perceived that the
moment he yielded either to grace or to weakness
the crisis ceased.[1] That the trial should end with the
soul's graceful decision did not surprise him so much

---

[1] It must be understood that here it is not a question of yielding
to *sin ;* ' weakness,' I take it, here means failure to respond to the
invitation of grace when the highest perfection is put before the
soul.

as the fact that he should be no longer tormented when he had decided according to self. It seemed to him as if the Beloved had appointed him to run in a number of races, each to be either won or lost ; and that success in one race did not mean that the remaining races could be foregone . . . it further appeared to him that there were some crises in the spiritual life which, when they had given place to quiet, could not be called either triumphs or failures : their issues were withheld from him. Now had the will been victorious and was the Beloved denying to the understanding the knowledge of its triumph ? Or had the will failed and was the devil nursing the defeat, ready to use it at a struggle yet to come ? '

So it will be seen that my author takes us not very much further in the matter, showing us only that the spiritual life must never be regarded as anything but a switchback of ups and downs, a course which is not only intended to be uneven but which is intended to defy the estimating of our progress on it. We are not meant to know, when we have turned a corner (or gone over a bump), whether we have been behaving correctly or clumsily : all that we are meant to learn from the experience is that there will be a lot more like it !

And so it was also with the people of Juda in the eighth and ninth century B.C. Nor, indeed, need we look to times so far removed from our own for the application of the above-suggested theory. Do we not see the same chances and the same dangers in the Zionist movement of to-day ? And when the movement has ceased to move—to be in turn succeeded by another—what, one wonders, will be advanced in accounting for its failure ? I suspect that any and

every argument will be brought forward before it is
suggested that the Chosen Race have never *really*
followed Isaias's advice . . . and that occasions for so
doing must recur until the end of time . . . whether at
any given crisis the Prophet's doctrine be followed or no.

vi

We have come now to the end of the eighth century
B.C. It is time we looked at Babylon.

Chaldea, even more than Egypt, had for generations
past represented the highest culture of the then known
world. The upstart Assyrians—upstart only in their
new-found empire—learned all they could from the
more polished race, making no secret of their admiration
for Babylonian learning and customs. It is thought,
for example, that the ' Assyrian altar ' which attracted
Achaz was really of Chaldean origin, and that the
' sun-dial of Achaz ' mentioned in Isaias xxxviii and
introduced at about the same time into Jerusalem is
to be attributed to the astronomical Babylonians.[1]
Even if these suggestions are without foundation it is
certain that the libraries of Nineveh were stocked with
Chaldean literature, and it is more than probable that
the school of scribes which was founded in Jerusalem
was employed in copying out Babylonian as well as
Hebrew ' sayings.'[2] But since we are considering

[1] It was the policy of the Assyrians to transplant a conquered
people into other non-Assyrian colonies, and so a Babylonian quarter
in a Samaritan town (with its own Babylonian altar) is just what
we would expect.

[2] ' Babylonia was the cradle of Assyrian culture and religion ;
it was the sacred motherland from which Asshur had gone forth in
prehistoric days to build the cities of Assyria. The Assyrian regarded
it as the mediæval German regarded Rome ; to be crowned king
at Babylon gave the Assyrian monarch the same title to veneration
that coronation at Rome gave to a Charlemagne or an Otho. It

Babylon rather from the military than from the academic standpoint it will be as well to turn at once to the leading figure of the Babylon of this period, the warlike Merodach-Baladan. This man, 'the son of Yagina,' was originally the chieftain of a tribe whose headquarters were in the marshland which lay about the northern banks of the Persian Gulf. Here, at the mouth of the Euphrates, with Elam on the east and Assyria on the north and west, Merodach-Baladan learned the arts of diplomacy and war. As early as 730 he seems to have been recognized by his country-men as the chosen deliverer of Babylon from the tyrannies of Assyria. Throughout Salmanasar's five years of reign Merodach-Baladan was consolidating his position and maintaining the practical independence of Chaldea. It was during Sargon's period of rule that Assyria concentrated its attention upon Babylon (710) with the result that Merodach-Baladan was forced to retire for a time to his estates at the mouth of the Euphrates. Five years later, when Sargon died, the chosen deliverer came out of hiding and staged a dramatic return to his capital. But this time he had not the assistance of his neighbours, the Elamites, to count upon. His reign lasted on this occasion exactly six months. Forced to spend the rest of his life in exile he was eventually tracked down on the coast of Elam by Sennacherib; this was in 697 B.C., after thirty-three years of stormy public life for the idealist prince, and it is recorded in the annals of Assyrian

was a visible sign of sovereignty in the valleys of the Tigris and the Euphrates, a proof that Bel had set apart the sovereign as the rightful successor of the heroes and princes of old. What the kings of the second Assyrian empire wanted in legitimacy of birth, they sought to obtain by the conquest of Babylon.' Sayce, *The Times of Isaiah*, p. 50.

history that Sennacherib found it as much as he could
do to effect the capture. It appears that he got
together a fleet of Phœnician seamen and, having
invoked the gods of the Persian Gulf, sailed to
Merodach-Baladan's coastal stronghold where he
sacked the town and slew the Babylonian fugitive.

One would have wished that Merodach-Baladan's
Elamite hosts had put up a better fight against Sennacherib, but they were an unreliable force at the best
of times and they had felt the edge of the Assyrian
sword before. Indeed one would have wished that
they had preserved for us at least a ' life story ' of
their distinguished guest, because all that has come
down to us is the fragmentary legend of a romantic
career. He is one of those picturesque figures that
find their way into the pages of Sacred Scripture
about which we would like to know a great deal more ;
he is a sort of Charles Stuart with a longer run for his
money—and with more money to do it on.

Now while all this was happening far away in the east,
Ezechias, almost at the western extremity of Assyria's
tribute kingdom, was hiring Arab mercenaries to
repair the damaged walls of Jerusalem, and to fortify
the city against possible attack from east or south.
Sennacherib was either too preoccupied—or else too
much disappointed by the mysterious reverses which
he had lately suffered in Juda—to put a stop to the
independent behaviour of Ezechias (who was still
technically his vassal) with the result that Juda's
morale was very distinctly stiffened. In Jerusalem
men were beginning to think that there was a lot to
be said for the Prophet Isaias after all . . . if his doctrine
of ' let be ' could be relied upon to produce such
beneficent results. With ramparts going up in every

direction one might comfortably trust in God ! I think I am right in quoting Queen Victoria as having said on the occasion of an accident threatening the royal carriage : ' I have had the wheels seen to, and the coachman is no fool, so there is nothing to do now but to rely on the help of Providence.'

Alas, the independence secured by Ezechias was destined to be of brief duration ! In the next reign, as we shall see, Juda found herself in harness once again. But at any rate for five years or so—before the end came to those fifteen years of life which had been added to him by the joint effect of his and the Prophet's prayer—the king was able to enjoy the peace for which his gentle nature craved. Ezechias died in 697, two years after the overthrow of Babylon at the hands of Sennacherib.

Thus at the end of the eighth century the only person who counts for anything as far as Juda is concerned is Sennacherib. Now this emperor seems to have fared worse at the hands of historians than ever he fared at the hands of his enemies. ' Brought up in the purple,' says the eminent Assyriologist, Dr. Sayce, ' Sennacherib soon showed that he was made of very different stuff from his father. Like the Persian Xerxes, he was weak and vainglorious, cowardly under reverse, cruel and boastful in success.' Far be it from an amateur like myself to doubt the word of the lifetime student, but I cannot help thinking that— seeing what the monarch in question accomplished in his time—the son was a fairly adequate successor to the father. If he was cowardly under reverse we have only one reverse to judge him by ; if he was cruel to Merodach-Baladan he was certainly showing himself to be unchivalrous but hardly untraditional . . . and if

he was boastful in success he was merely echoing the
phrases in which all previous Assyrian records had been
couched. Sennacherib is not one of the five great men
whom I would select from history to picnic with me on
the downs (what possibilities the thought suggests!), but
I fail to see why Sargon should be any more acceptable.

With Assyria employed in the regions of the Tigris
and Euphrates, the land about the Jordan was able
to take upon itself a more rural and less martial
character. The capital might look to its defences, but
the country had best concentrate on agriculture.
This, at any rate, was the advice of Isaias. There
seems to be more than a casual connection between
the Prophet's belief in husbandry and his belief in the
Messianic remnant ; it is almost as if he identifies the
two in some way, wishing his chosen ones to sanctify
themselves by toil in preparation for the coming of
Him who should be the Fruit of the Harvest. With
the fall of Adam came the burden of work, with the
birth of Christ comes its reward. ' As the rain and
the snow come down from heaven and return no
more thither but soak the earth and water it, and make
it to spring and give seed to the sower and bread to
the eater, so shall My Word be which shall go forth
from My mouth ; it shall not return to Me void but
shall do whatsoever I please and shall prosper in the
things for which I sent it. For you shall go out with
joy and be led forth with peace ; the mountains and
the hills shall sing praise before you and all the trees
of the country shall clap their hands. Instead of the
shrub shall come up the fir-tree, and instead of the
nettle shall come up the myrtle-tree ; and the Lord
shall be named for an everlasting sign that shall not
be taken away.'

vii

All during this period, the last few years of Ezechias's
reign, Isaias employed himself in preparing Juda for
the ' scourge ' which he had heralded in less clearly
defined terms thirty years before.   While from his
earlier sermons the people of Jerusalem had understood the Prophet to mean that Assyria would ultimately wipe out all but the very few, they now saw that
it was Babylon, not Nineveh, to which they were
destined to be led in chains. Assyria had served God's
purpose in keeping Juda in a state of fear and con-
sequent dependence upon Him, but it was to be
Chaldea that should lead the Chosen People into that
captivity from which Cyrus—a type of the deliverer,
Christ—was to free them after seventy years of bitter
humiliation.   The sweep of the Prophet's vision is
indeed immense ! One by one he deals with the
destinies of Assyria, Philistia, Moab, Syria and
Samaria, Egypt and Ethiopia, Tyre, and now at last
Babylon, the most formidable of them all. He sees
that Nabuchodonosor is more of a danger to Juda
than Sennacherib ever was ; he sees even further
than this—he sees beyond the destruction of Babylon
itself. And how graphic is Isaias in the telling of it ,
' Behold this man cometh, the rider upon the chariot
with two horsemen [the Medes and the Persians] and
he answered and said : Babylon is fallen, she is fallen ;
and all the graven gods thereof are broken unto the
ground.' But you must read ch. xxi to get the swing
of it . . . and then go straight on to xlv, xlvi, and xlvii
where Isaias seems to lose all sense of time, and where
he sings so rapturously of the ' anointed Cyrus ' that
it is almost impossible to make out where he is referring

to the noble Persian and where to Christ. To me personally—and I ask no more of the reader than to listen to me saying so—the prophecy about Cyrus as the mystical forerunner of Our Lord (xlv) is by far the most appealing of all Isaias's prophecies. It is in this chapter that the verse occurs which souls may cling to when every other text in Holy Scripture seems to defy interpretation : ' Verily thou art a hidden God, the God of Israel the Saviour.' However thick our darkness there is always that ! When words have ceased to mean anything, when pain and disappointment have robbed us of the last vestige of desire, when creatures have demanded of us what little we have reserved in the recesses of our souls for God . . . ' verily a hidden God ' is He in Whose service we are enrolled. And surely by the time we have come to the end of the same forty-fifth chapter we shall begin to appreciate again—not to *feel*, but, in some sort and perhaps inadequately, to *know*—that ' there is no God else besides Me . . . for I am God and there is no other . . . therefore he shall say : In the Lord are my justices and empire ; they shall come to Him and all that resist Him shall be confounded ; in the Lord shall all the seed of Israel be justified and praised.'

.   .   .   .   .   .

' And Ezechias slept with his fathers, and Manasses his son reigned in his stead.'

H

CHAPTER VI

IN MANASSES'S REIGN

'IN Judea, of S. Isaias the Prophet, who under King
Manasses was slain by being sawn asunder, and is
buried under the oak of Rogel by the crossing of the
waters.' I quote this from the Roman Martyrology
which gives to our Prophet a feast-day on July 6th.
This chapter will add little to what has gone before,
but I have wanted to make it clear that I am not
alone in adhering to the 'legend' of the Prophet's
death. The sawing asunder makes a far more suitable
finish to the Prophet's career than the lingering on to
a disappointed old age in Manasses's reign, and even
if he never reached the period with which we are about
to deal, I find it hard to picture Isaias suffering the
petty humiliations, earlier in the century, of a well-
cushioned decline. It used to be a favourite joke
among Scripture students that whether or not Isaias
had been sawn asunder by Manasses he had certainly
been so dealt with by the critics! But as I have not
dared to venture upon the question of the 'first' and
'second' Isaias in the foregoing pages, I suppose I
have no right to quote the jest. The arguments for
and against the integrity of Isaias are briefly given
in Father Pope's 'Aids' to the Bible, Vol. II, p.
299 f., so I shall not add more to the already incredible
amount of writing that goes to the confusion of this
point.

Leaving, then, the identity of the ' deutero ' Isaias to the higher critics, and shelving the question of the Prophet's death until all these things are made clear for us in the light of Eternal Glory, it is only right that we should pursue the course of Juda's history in relation to the nations round about for just so long as it is possible that Isaias *might* have lived—to the close, that is, of Manasses's active period.

Since of all the peoples that have occupied us hitherto it is the Assyrians who have claimed the most attention, it must be the story of Assyria that we should consider first in any survey of Manasses's reign.

If Manasses came to the throne of Juda in 697 B.C., then Sennacherib had still another sixteen years of rule after the death of his one successful enemy, Ezechias. We do not know exactly on what terms were Sennacherib and the king of Juda when once the vassal had asserted himself, but it is noticeable that the policy of Assyria towards her dependents underwent a change at about this time. The transplanting of conquered races to other dominions within the empire had not reduced the colonial kingdom to the unity which had been aimed at by Theglathphalasar ; some form of meeting native governments half-way had to be found if local rebellions were to be avoided. And local rebellions could be all too troublesome in such a scattered empire as was that of Assyria. With the memory of King Osee's behaviour in Israel still green in the mind of Sennacherib it was not likely that the system of allowing native rulers to govern dependent states should have recommended itself ; Sennacherib relied upon conquest rather than upon conciliation. But when Sennacherib was murdered in 681 by two of his sons a more lenient administration

was resorted to—and with conspicuous success—by his
third son and successor, Asarhaddon.

Throughout the reign of Asarhaddon there seems to
have been little in the way of disaffection on the part
of tribute nations. Wherever possible Assyrian satraps
were removed from office and members of the old royal
lines were reinstated. Freedom of worship was
granted ; old customs were revived that had been
abolished by either Sargon or Sennacherib ; national
governments were allowed to resume their functions
on old constitutional lines ; the distinctive life of each
conquered people was encouraged to develop along its
own traditional course. Now how did all this effect
Juda ?

The period of liberty which we have noted as coming
to Juda during the last years of Ezechias was, as we
have suggested, destined to be short-lived ; early in
Manasses's reign Sennacherib must have tightened the
hold on Juda, because (though we hear no more of the
Assyrian conqueror's activities as regards Jerusalem)
there is evidence that Manasses made a bid for complete
independence and was flung into prison for doing so.
It had been one thing for Ezechias to show fight to a
hostile Sennacherib, but it was quite another for
Manasses to raise his voice against a quiescent lord ;
Isaias could well defend the former action but he would
never have sanctioned the latter ' . . . see thou be
quiet. . . .' (Indeed it may have been this insistence
on a passive attitude in the face of the king's desire
for war that cost the Prophet his life ; *if*, that is, he
was still alive by then.) Whether or not Manasses was
buoyed up in his ambitious schemes by the thought of
his father's success, his resistance came to nought ;
Juda was made subject once more.

But Asarhaddon's policy favoured Manasses ; the rebel was relieved of his chains and sent back to govern Juda. He did not rebel again. In fact it must soon have become obvious to the hot-headed Manasses that he and his country were far safer under Asarhaddon than they were likely to be if they were completely on their own ; all he had to do was to acknowledge a supremacy which had now been making itself felt with more or less intensity for four generations, and agree to let Asarhaddon use Jerusalem as the base of any operations he might undertake against Egypt. A paragraph will be devoted below to the war between Assyria and Egypt, so we can conclude this section with a summing up of Asarhaddon's reign and general influence.

Stepping, so to speak, over pools of his father's blood, the first thing that he did when he sat upon the empty throne was to get rid of his brothers and their allies. It had not been affection for himself that had prompted his father's murder, and Asarhaddon knew his family well enough to judge of his chances— and those of his people—if the assassination were to go unavenged. Armenia, with two Assyrian princes to swell her armies, was a dangerous neighbour. The conquest of Armenia was the first of Asarhaddon's signal triumphs.

In the previous reign, after Sennacherib had driven the Chaldean patriot into exile, Babylon had been levelled to the ground and the ruins of that once beautiful city had been used to dam the river Araxes. Asarhaddon built it up again. And, what is more, he seems to have endeared himself in some sort to the crushed and battered Babylonians. The city became the centre of Assyrian and Chaldean trade, second only

in rank to Nineveh itself. Asarhaddon died in 668
B.C., after a reign of thirteen years, and was succeeded
by his son Assurbanipal.

As hinted above, the matter that engaged Asarhaddon's energies during most of his period of rule
was the revival of power in Egypt. Isaias foresaw the
clash of these two rival forces (xix), but there must
have been very few in the Palestine of that time who
would have been prepared to predict a recovery from
Egypt's defeat at Eltekeh. And as a fact it was not
Egypt as a nation, but Egypt as a jig-saw of dependent
protectorates, that rose against the suzerain Assyria.
Every now and again the defeated Ethiopian warrior,
Tirhaka, would come out of his hiding in the south
and fan the disaffection into flame ; he hoped, probably,
that if once a general and united insurrection could be
got under way the national spirit of the Egyptians
would be found strong enough to oust the Assyrian
deputies altogether. How far the semi-detached
states of Egypt clung together we do not know, but
certain it is that Egypt as a whole made matters so
difficult for Asarhaddon that he decided to launch his
attack upon that nation in a way which would leave
no room for further enterprise on Egypt's part ; he
would not halt at Raphia (as his grandfather, Sargon,
had done) nor yet at Eltekeh (as his father, Sennacherib, had done twenty years later), he would press
on until he came to Thebes . . . and reduce it to a heap
of ashes.[1] But as a fact he never lived to see the finish
of his Egyptian campaign ; he had reduced Egypt

[1] The two previous conquerors seem to have satisfied themselves
as to Egypt's dependency by the imposition of a tribute ; neither
men penetrated in person into the country they intended to colonize.
I cannot account for this, unless perhaps it was that they were too
busy !

to dependence by 672, but it was left to his son, Assurbanipal, to inflict the final blows upon the conquered nation ; Thebes was not destroyed until 666.

Before he died Asarhaddon had at least the satisfaction of taking Tirhaka prisoner, though, strange to say, he did not have him executed. One wonders if the magnanimous Assyrian still had hopes of being able to use the Ethiopian as a dependent governor ? Such a course would have been quite in keeping with his policy of native rule, but even Asarhaddon must have been loth to experiment with an ex-sovereign who had had such an exciting past. There is an interesting bas-relief in the Berlin Museum (reproduced in Professor Lods' *Prophets and the Rise of Judaism,* p. 30) which shows Asarhaddon interviewing two conquered chieftains ; the Assyrian is standing erect and the two diminutive figures are looking up at their suzerain who holds them captive by a cord which they appear to be in the act of swallowing.[1] The negro-like features of the larger prisoner are taken to mean that this is none other than our friend Tirhaka, while the other, the more insignificant of the two, is identified as Ba'alu, king of Tyre, who is known to have been in league with Tirhaka at about this time. The inscription which accompanies the piece of sculpture gives an account of the fall of Memphis, which took place probably about a year before Asarhaddon's death.

[1] Perhaps an explanation of this form of servitude may be found in the words of Isaias xxxvii, 29, where the Prophet says that the Lord will ' put a ring in thy nose, and a bit between thy lips, and I will turn thee back by the way by which thou camest.' Many of the passages which, on a casual glance at the Prophecy, appear to be figurative, have, when one comes to look at the footnotes of such commentaries as Cheyne's or Skinner's, a strictly literal sense.

Whether Ba'alu, Tirhaka's fellow-conspirator,[1] escaped
the death that he deserved we do not know, but
certainly Tirhaka appeared again under Assurbanipal
as leader of the injured race.

What a hopeful person Tirhaka must have been !
He even seems to have justified some of his hopes ;
Memphis, according to some authorities,[2] opened its
doors to the Ethiopian, and, for a little while, even the
power of Assyria was helpless in the face of the patriotic
enthusiasm which the man inspired. But Memphis
fell a second time ; Assurbanipal, reinforced from the
north, drove Tirhaka back into his own country to
Napata, the capital of Ethiopia, but even then, driven
to the last extremity, the extraordinary southerner
managed to retain his kingship. He made one more effort
to regain Memphis and, when this failed, retreated into
the Soudan where he died after a reign of twenty-five
years. Had he lived one more year he would have
seen the devastation of Thebes ; at least the old man
was spared that.[3]

The sacking of Thebes was considered a piece of
outrageous vandalism even for those rough days. Loot
in the shape of temple statuary was sent home to
Nineveh, and what could not be removed was destroyed.
The palaces and temples for which Thebes had been
famous were not even able, in the same generation, to
provide a shelter for cattle ; with the result that when
the Egyptians managed to shake off the Assyrian yoke
a few years later it was not at Thebes but in the Delta

---

[1] According to Budge, *History of Esarhaddon*, p. 114 (quoted by
Driver, *Isaiah*), it was Ba'alu who was responsible for the outbreak
against Assyria, Tirhaka being called in to put the finishing touches
to the movement.

[2] See Sayce, op. cit., p. 35.

[3] An interesting head of Tirhaka is reproduced in Sir W. Flinders-
Petrie's admirable work, *Egypt and Israel*, p. 76.

that the nation's centre was established. This, however, is taking us into what corresponds to the latter
part of Manasses's reign—the period to which even I
would not assign the Prophet's closing years—and so
forms no part of the present study. This much,
nevertheless, can be added before leaving Assyria for
good and all : that during the first part of Manasses's
reign, from 697 until roughly about 680, Assyria was
attaining to the height of its power and influence ;
literature and art were being encouraged with the
best results, and it would have been impossible to
foresee at that time, or indeed at any time during
Manasses's reign, that the supremacy of Assyria
would so soon pass into the hands of the Neo-Baby-
lonian Empire ; which it did in 625. But Isaias
foresaw it clearly enough !

When Assyria was at its best Juda was at its worst :
Manasses did not scruple to undo all the good that his
father had done. With Assyrian soldiery billeted in
the Holy City it is perhaps understandable that the
morals of Juda should decline ; with a weak—and I
sometimes think a half mad—king upon the throne,
it is perhaps understandable that public opinion should
make no objection to the increase of idolatrous
practices . . . but even so ! And it is not as if God
were leaving them to manage as best they could ; He
seems to have warned them in the plainest terms :
' in the hand of His servants the prophets, saying :
Because Manasses king of Juda hath done these most
wicked abominations beyond all that the Amorrhites
did before him and hath made Juda also to sin with
his filthy doings, therefore thus saith the Lord the
God of Israel : Behold I will bring evils upon Jerusalem and Juda, that whosoever shall hear of them,

both his ears shall tingle.' One wonders who these ' prophets ' were that issued this message from the Lord ; were they the disciples of Isaias ? The chosen ones who were to be the nucleus of the ' remnant ' ? They were brave men whoever they were, because ' Manasses shed very much innocent blood, till he filled Jerusalem up to the mouth.' The Book of Kings (from which these quotations are being taken : IV, xxi) is positively shocked at the wickedness of Manasses ; again and again ' the evil which he did in the sight of the Lord ' is returned to. Woe, woe, woe, if Isaias is still alive for all this ! But since there is not a word about the king in the Prophet's book he cannot have had to endure the prevailing abuses for long. Imagine the Isaias whom we have followed throughout this book submitting to a tyranny far more deadly than any that had threatened from hostile powers ; imagine him watching pagan altars being built in the House of the Lord[1] . . . no, we must not make the Prophet die of a broken heart, a broken body is quite enough.

Isaias has done his work ; and there are ' prophets ' to continue what he has done. Just as he was seldom listened to in his lifetime so now also his tradition is rejected. What a perfect summing up of the prophetical vocation are the words which we have remembered from Isaias's original call and the words which tell of the spirit he left behind him ! ' And the Lord said : Go, and thou shalt say to this people : Hearing, hear and understand not ; and see the vision, and know it not. Blind the heart of this people, and make their ears heavy, and shut their eyes ; lest they see with their eyes and hear with their ears, and be converted.'

[1] 4 Kings xxi, 5.

Strictly indeed has it been fulfilled ! What a melancholy task he has had to do ! But not more melancholy than what those had to do who were to continue his traditions : ' The Lord spoke in the hands of His prophets . . . but they [the people] hearkened not, but were seduced by Manasses to do evil more than the nations which the Lord destroyed before the children of Israel.'

All through the pages of Sacred Scripture it is everywhere the same : heroic effort . . . dismal failure. And not in Sacred Scripture alone but in the lives also of the saints. Has not every apostle, and every prophet, and every reformer, been given a light to guide him which has—as far as he can see—sooner or later fizzled out ? But the point is *he has gone on as if it were still there.* And as a matter of fact, of course, it *is* still there. ' In darkness shall thy light rise up.'[1] But the saint is not meant to see it, or feel its warmth.

And how about those who, on his account, ' shut their eyes, and stop their ears, and harden their hearts, lest they be converted and God should heal them ' ? Is the saint responsible for these ? O reader, reader, even if you put down this book having derived no other thought from it but this, I pray you respect the doctrine of the closing page : in the Person of Christ it was said of the saint—be he prophet or preacher or merely the man of prayer—' Behold this Child is set for the fall and for the resurrection of many in Israel, and for a sign which shall be contradicted.'

Prophecy, sanctity, prayer . . . so many signs that the world must ever contradict. The world knows its own, and these are not of the world. Fortunate, indeed, if the gainsaying come with a sword instead

[1] lviii, 10.

of with a sneer. But sword or sneer, the Prophet
Isaias received his share of contradiction. Prophets
come to their own, and their own receive them not.
Just as Isaias ' walked naked and barefoot three
years '[1] in witness to the truth, so Christ whom he
heralded preached for three years in Juda . . . and
then was ' contradicted '—unto death.

And all the time Isaias *knew he was going to be
contradicted* . . . for just so long as he should raise
his voice in the uttering of the Word ; contradicted,
moreover, on the one subject on which he possessed
expert and inside knowledge. Hard, was it not ?
And the Prophet's whole life was spent under that
cloud : the cloud that hung over Christ—with even
greater weight—from Bethlehem to Gethsemane. Oh,
no, dear reader, Isaias was not ' mercifully blinded '
(as some have seemed to think) on the day that he
received the call to preach ; rather, he blinded himself
to the pains which such a mission should involve . . .
accepting open-eyed the need to suffer. ' I will not
count the cost,' Isaias seems to say, ' lest I feel, in
my poverty, that sanctity is too expensive ; nor will
I regard the task itself, lest my eyes turn back again
upon my impotence. What then ? This will I do :
I will give myself without reserve ; I will " wait for
His word . . . be quiet . . . and God Himself will come
and save me." '[2]

Thus it is, surely, that for Isaias the sum of man's
duty—nay, the perfection of man's sanctity—consists
in a willingness to be guided by the Providence of
God . . . a Providence whose decrees appear to be
fortuitous ! ' Wait . . . be quiet . . . He will save.'
Patience, docility, generosity with God. Oh, the more

[1] xx, 2, 3.   [2] viii, 17 ; vii, 4 ; xxxv, 4.

we read the Gospels and the Prophets the more must
we realize that the one indispensable condition of all
holiness is generosity. Teach us, Lord, only how to
love, and the rest will look after itself. Our love will
find expression in surrender—a giving which can stop
at nothing but the emptying of self—until we can say
with the Prophet, 'Lo, here am I, send me.' Send
me, Lord, to any work of Thine, 'for *Thou* wilt bring
forth a seed out of Jacob, and out of Juda a possessor
of Thy mountains.'[1]

[1] lxv, 9.

APPENDIX I

To anyone familiar with the period it must appear that I have skated very thinly over one portion of the surface —the part dealing with Sennacherib's invasion of Juda and his subsequent defeat. The reason why I have, except for the briefest references, reserved the matter for an appendix is twofold : first, because almost every authority has his own rendering of what occurred ; and second, because apart from the verses I have quoted in the text, information regarding the event is wholly derived from non-Isaian sources. In choosing to follow one writer rather than summarize the evidence of many I am presuming to use for the substance of this appendix the seventh chapter of Driver's *Isaiah ;* it seems to me to give a clearer account than any other I have come across.

In 701 (according to Assyrian monuments) the emperor Sennacherib, after a successful campaign against Sidon and Phœnicia, marched against Juda. Surrounding Jerusalem, he had Ezechias—to use the words of the inscription—' shut up as a bird in a cage.' The case for Jerusalem must have looked just then as hopeless as it could possibly be : Egypt—even allowing that she would be prepared to send a relieving force (which, in fact, she did)—was a long way off and had, between herself and Jerusalem, Sennacherib's southern army to contend against before ever there could be question of breaking the Assyrian line that was drawn around the Holy City. But though the situation seemed desperate—perhaps because of it— Isaias's prophecies of about this time are remarkable for their almost boisterous confidence. Chapters x and xi belong to this period, their keynote being : ' O My people that

dwellest in Sion, be not afraid of the Assyrian ; he shall
strike thee with his rod, and he shall lift up his staff over
thee in the way of Egypt . . . and the Lord of Hosts shall
raise up a scourge against him . . . and it shall come to
pass in that day that his burden shall be taken away from
off thy shoulder, and his yoke from off thy neck, and the
yoke shall putrify at the presence of the oil.' Nothing shall
be left of the forest of Assyria, Isaias promises, but a few
charred stumps, for ' the Light of Israel shall be as a fire,
and the Holy One thereof as a flame . . . and his thorns
and briers shall be set on fire, and shall be devoured in one
day.' Isaias is reminding the Hebrews that their view of
the wood is being hindered by their (mistaken) conception
of the trees ! This impending calamity is nothing more nor
less than what has been foretold : Assyria is the scourge of
God's choosing . . . Assyria must never again be looked to for
protection . . . *and* the calamity shall suddenly pass away.

A little difficulty presents itself here by reason of the
fact that Isaias seems to see Sennacherib arriving in force
from the north whereas the invaders in fact came up from
the south-west. It may be that the Prophet, high up on
his watch-tower and in labour with his inspiration, paid
little attention to the points of the compass (after all, it
was no part of his ' burden ' to indicate the direction of the
enemy's advance), or perhaps Isaias was considering the
present evil as something emanating in the north no
matter whence its attack should ultimately be made. At
any rate the detail makes not the smallest difference,
while it is quite within the bounds of possibility that some
tablet will one day come to light showing Isaias to have
been perfectly right, and that one of the detachments of
Assyria's army *did* storm Jerusalem from the north. I
do not say that such a discovery is likely, but it is the kind
of thing that is constantly taking place—to the exquisite
mortification of the critics. However this may be, the
main business of the campaign was certainly conducted on
the south side of the city.

Sennacherib thought it better to subdue the Philistine cities first of all, before fixing his whole attention upon the wiping out of Juda. Engaged thus with Ascalon and Ekron he sent a second, and a smaller, army (under Rabsaces) to harry the land of the Israelites. This is Driver's account; he puts it more eloquently than I could do:

'At the same time Juda was overrun by the Assyrian soldiery; forty-six strong cities and many smaller places were captured; more than 200,000 inhabitants, with their possessions, carried off as spoil. The territory of Judah can never before have suffered so terribly. Isaiah had truly foretold that, though the nation might escape eventually, it would escape only after great trouble and disaster. Meanwhile Jerusalem itself was blockaded; the captured cities, with their territory, were distributed amongst the three Philistine kings, the king of Ashdod, the king of Ekron, and the king of Gaza, who had remained loyal to Assyria. At this point Hezekiah appears to have made the effort of submission recorded in 2 Kings xviii, 14,[1] "I have offended; return from me; that which thou puttest upon me I will bear," accompanied doubtless by promises of obedience for the future. The offer was accepted; according to the inscription, an immense and, in some items, hardly credible tribute was imposed, consisting not only in heavy payment of gold and silver, but in an enormous amount of other valuables as well. It is even added that Hezekiah's daughters and the women of his palace were sent after the Great King to Nineveh.'

Professor Lods, in his *Prophets and the Rise of Judaism*, reproduces a bas-relief, which is now in the British Museum, showing Sennacherib at Lachis receiving tribute from large numbers of Hebrew and Philistine prisoners; the trees depicted in the upper part of the design, and the horses

[1] In our version it is, of course, the Fourth, not the Second Book of Kings.

and chariots which fill up the space below the royal throne,
are peculiarly—though unconsciously—appropriate when
we remember all that Isaias has to say of Assyrian forests
and Assyrian cavalry.

  Thus with almost the whole of Palestine at Sennacherib's
feet it is indeed wonderful to find that Isaias can still
reassert the imminence of Assyria's downfall.   Read xiv,
24–27, and again xvii and xviii (which are too long to
quote here in their entirety), and marvel at the Prophet's
confidence.   By now Jerusalem is apparently aware of
Egypt's decision to come to the Holy City's assistance ;
Isaias rejects the proffered hand !   By all means let the
Ethiopian hasten to Jerusalem's gates, but not in order to
attack the besieger so much as to witness the triumph of
the besieged (xviii, 1–5).   Again to quote Dr. Driver :
' Some circumstance occurred, either arousing Sennacherib's suspicion, or making him dissatisfied with the
engagement which he had concluded.   It may be that
news reached him of warlike preparations being still
carried on in Jerusalem, or he may have heard of a fresh
movement on the part of the Egyptian forces (which, in
fact, soon actually took place—ch. xxxvii, 9), and may
have begun to feel that he had been guilty of a strategical
error in leaving a strong fortress like Jerusalem unreduced
in his rear ;   whatever the motive,[1] a fresh demand was
now made by him for the unconditional surrender of the
capital.'

  In Isaias xxxiii we find the Prophet pouring oil on the
frenzied waters of Jerusalem ;   he tells his hearers that he
already *sees* the turn of fortune . . . why will they not
trust ?   This is the stage at which the Rabsaces mission
takes place, and where Ezechias makes his supreme act
of faith in God and in the trustworthiness of his Prophet.
But we have dealt with this very fully above.

  The firm line taken by Isaias restores in some sort the

  [1] It is implied by Isaias (' he hath broken the covenant,' xxxiii, 8)
that the demand involved a breach of faith.

  I

confidence of the masses ; they watch Rabsaces retire
from the city gates and they seem to make no further
moan against the course of defiance. What prevents
Rabsaces from attacking there and then ? With Egypt
making forced marches from the south he would do well,
it might be suggested, to storm the citadel at once. For
one thing Rabsaces's army was probably too small for this,
and for another, he was only an envoy, and had doubtless
to inform his chief before daring to act on the results of
his parley.

Meanwhile Sennacherib has left Lachis for Libna (which
is even closer to Jerusalem) where he begins to make
preparations for Tirhaka's approach. We can imagine the
kind of thing that must have been said in the ' bird-cage '
fortress of Jerusalem : Tirhaka cannot possibly know the
strength of Sennacherib's army, reinforced as it is by the
troops which he has made his own in the earlier part of
the campaign . . . would it be any good attempting a sortie ?
. . . allowing that our walls will stand any amount of batter-
ing, how long can we manage without food procured from
outside ? . . . the merest handful of Assyrians (or a few
deserters) could cut off Jerusalem's water supply in a single
night. . . .

And then, when it must have seemed to all alike—Jews,
Assyrians, Philistines (what was left of them), and the
advance guard of the Egyptians—that the history of the
Chosen People was as good as closed, when Sion is humbled,
destitute, and has (except for Isaias who is positively
exultant over the anticipated defeat of Assyria : xxxvii,
22–35) reached rock-bottom, *then* comes the dramatic
somersault of fortune . . . ' and the flower of Assyria is cut
off.' We know from the passage in Kings already quoted
in the text what actually took place. Whatever may be
advanced by unbelieving critics, the thing is as supernatural
as anything that has ever happened in history. Even
Sennacherib is silent as to the cause of his ' retirement '
from the theatre of war. Egypt, it is true, records a

different version of the story from that which is found in
the Book of Kings, but even here we find that the strictly-
miraculous is given as a reason for Assyria's defeat . . .
though it is on behalf of Egypt and due to Egypt's devotion
that the ' miracle ' is worked ! This is out of our province
and so I shall not add to this already lengthy Appendix
with an account of what Egypt thought about the matter,
but for those who will pursue Egypt's considerations (as
revealed to Herodotus by the guides who showed him the
antiquities of Memphis) there is a page or two devoted to
them in Sayce's *Times of Isaiah*, ch. II.

APPENDIX II

In the earlier part of this book Isaias has been dealt with rather roughly as a social reformer ; the reason for not treating of this aspect of his work in greater detail is simply this : I have said so much about ' prevalent abuses ' when describing the activities of the Minor Prophets that I feel half ashamed of using all the old phrases again ! Conscious, however, that this is no valid excuse for the omission I am trying to make good in an appendix. But my intention here is to approach the social reform programme from a new angle—new, that is, to my particular study of the prophets—and to show what Isaias hoped the people of Jerusalem would do, rather than to stress, by fishing indictments from my prophetical stock-pot, what the Prophet objected to.

As a purely social reformer, then, the aim of Isaias seems to have been to get the people back to the land. It is much what some are trying to do to-day ; where other generations of prophets have taken for their sermons the Sins of Society, the modern Isaiases (Father Vincent McNabb, for instance) are aptly pointing to the Treasure which lies hidden in the Field. It will be as well, therefore, for us who are suffering from the evils of Industrialism to turn up some of the Prophet's more trenchant statements on the subject of husbandry, and to devote to the ' land-development texts ' the space which I shrank from giving in the body of the book.

First of all, and in general, we can note that it is by no means an unusual thing for a prophet to use the phraseology of the nature-lover, but the reason why such images as we find in Isaias are employed by most of the prophets is usually because the farm or the hill-side has been the scene of their home lives ; to Isaias, however, a king was probably a more familiar figure than a cow, and so if, as is the case, the Prophet borrows his pictures from the country life of Palestine it is because he wants to point a lesson, and not merely because he wants to reminisce about the old days on the farm . . .

It is in ch. xxviii that the ideals of husbandry are first held out to the people of Jerusalem ; the occasion seems to have been the threatening of Samaria by Salmanasar. Isaias turns from his description of Israel's sin to point to similar evils within the borders of Juda, and then winds up his discourse with a homily about the perseverance which is required for the work of agriculture. At first sight the connection with what has just gone before is obscure, but when one looks into it the Prophet is obviously moralizing thus : You suffer at the hands of your neighbours . . . and well do you deserve so to suffer . . . but even had your sins not merited rough treatment you would know from your tending of the crops that violent measures and heroic endurance are often necessary to obtain the right results . . . a pity, indeed, that you do not pay more attention to the farmyard and less to the council-chamber . . . you would be readier to keep the *end* in view. ' For He will instruct him in judgement, his God will teach him.' This is surely intended to show the Jews that just as the farmer treats his ground and his seeds in a way which seems destructive to the ordinary eye, so the Lord deals out severity to those of whom He expects an abundant harvest. See, there is a purpose in it all ! ' For gith shall not be thrashed with saws, neither shall the cart-wheel turn about upon the cummin ; but gith shall be beaten out with a rod, and cummin with a staff. But bread-corn shall be broken small ; but the thrasher shall not thrash it for ever, neither shall the cart-wheel hurt it, nor break it with its teeth. This also is come forth from the Lord God of hosts to make His counsel wonderful and magnify justice.'

Thus it is that, in future, whenever Isaias is talking about the Messias or about the ' remnant,' he reverts to the particular kind of labour that is to occupy the re-modelled society. ' I will open rivers in the high hills, and fountains in the midst of the plains, I will turn the desert into pools of waters and the impassible land into streams of waters. I will plant in the wilderness the cedar, the thorn, the myrtle, and the olive-tree ; I will set in the desert the fir-tree, the elm, and the box-tree together ... that they may *see*, and *know*, and *consider*, and *under-stand*. . . .' This is how the Lord prepares His ground ; and now, when all is ready : ' Let the earth be opened and bud forth a Saviour.' It is when the Saviour has estab-lished Himself that the Lord can say to man : ' Come forth, and to them that are in darkness : Show yourselves. They shall be fed in the ways, *and their pastures shall be in every plain.*' Lastly there is that verse which hints at such an abundance of prosperity that even the burdens of agriculture will pass away : ' strangers shall be your husbandmen, and the dressers of your vines.' But it is the field and the vine, nevertheless, that spell this happi-ness ; bartering in the bazaar will never bring such plenty. ' For as the earth bringeth forth her bud, and as the garden causeth her seed to shoot forth, so shall the Lord God make justice to spring forth, and praise before all nations.' ' Surely I will no more give thy corn to be meat for thy enemies ; and the sons of strangers shall no more drink thy wine for which thou hast laboured. For they that gather it shall eat it and shall praise the Lord, and they that bring it together shall drink it in My holy courts '— the Prophet seems to have forgotten about strangers doing the rough work for them—' and the plains shall be turned to folds of flocks,' he continues a little farther on, ' and the valley of Achor into a place for the herds to lie down in. . . .' Why all this bliss, you ask ? And for whom ? The answer is in the same verse (lxv, 10) : ' For My people that have sought Me.'

S. James sums up the Prophet's thought when he says at the close of his Epistle : ' Be patient, therefore, brethren, until the coming of the Lord. Behold the husbandman waiteth for the precious fruit of the earth, patiently bearing until he receive the early and the latter rain. Be you therefore patient also, and strengthen your hearts ; for the coming of the Lord is at hand.'[1]

[1] James v, 7, 8.